SLIMMING
MAGAZINE

MICROWAVE
AND
FREEZER
LOW CALORIE RECIPE BOOK

ARGUS BOOKS

Editor: Sybil Greatbatch
Senior Home Economist:
Glynis McGuinness
Design: Carolyne Sibley

First published by Argus Books 1990
Argus House
Boundary Way
Hemel Hempstead
Herts HP2 7ST
England

Copyright © Slimming Magazine 1990

ISBN 1 85486 037 2

Printed and bound in Great Britain by
Clays Ltd, St Ives plc.

This book is sold subject to the condition that it shall not, by way of trade or otherwise, be lent, re-sold, hired out or otherwise circulated without the publisher's prior consent in any form of binding or cover other than that in which it is published and without a similar condition including this condition being imposed on the subsequent purchaser.

CONTENTS

Year by year, Slimming Magazine's reputation has grown as the world's leader in its field. This success is based on one editorial aim: to be the best friend a dieter ever had . . . a friend who is understanding, honest, sensible — and fun. And supremely well informed. Slimming Magazine is able to advise on diet and nutrition with all the authority of an internationally respected scientific team. Its very human experts also have an unrivalled insight into the practical problems of dieting: they have suffered themselves!

INTRODUCTION

What's the most successful diet plan you can follow? The answer to that question is usually the plan that fits most easily into your lifestyle. And if while you are dieting you discover some new ways of cooking delicious meals that are low in calories, then it will be far easier to keep slim once you reach target weight. In this book you'll find lots of recipes that will fit into any dieting allowance.

How a microwave can help you to slim

Whether you cook your meals in the microwave or use it for reheating meals from the freezer, you can be sure that you won't have to wait very long for a diet meal to be ready. And that could save you nibbling away at whatever is handy in your kitchen while you wait. Even if you are cooking higher-calorie meals for the whole family it is easy to do just-for-one low calorie alternatives for yourself in minutes in a microwave. Most of the recipes in the microwave section of this book are for one portion. So you need never worry about leftover portions tempting you to eat more than you really intend.

All the recipes have been tested in a 600 watt cooker with a turntable. If your cooker doesn't have a turntable you will need to turn the dish a few times during cooking. If your cooker is 750, 700 or 650 watts you will need to reduce the cooking time slightly, and if it is 500 watts you will need to increase the time.

It is important to weigh ingredients accurately, partly because that way you will know exactly how many calories your dish contains, but also quantity will affect the cooking times. The weights given for ingredients such as potatoes, carrots, etc, are peeled weights. And you should weigh meat after you have trimmed off any fat or gristle. Where the recipe asks you to cover the dish, use a fairly close-fitting lid or film. If you use film remember to pierce it a couple of times to prevent ballooning. Always prick foods that are cooked in their skins, such as potatoes and aubergines, to prevent them bursting. Many of the recipes have serving suggestions and you can use your microwave to cook vegetable accompaniments. On page 70 you'll find timings for average portions and their calories, too. When reheating food in a microwave make sure that it is heated all the way through. Soups and casseroles should always be stirred part way through cooking. A microwave thermometer is a useful aid for checking that the correct temperature has been reached. A ready-prepared dish being reheated should register at least 65 °C after taking it from the microwave and after a few minutes standing time that temperature should then rise to about 72 °C.

How your freezer can help you to slim

All the recipes in the freezer section make at least eight portions so that you can stock up your freezer with dieting meals when you begin a weight loss campaign. Plan to have a big cook-in and you could easily stack your freezer with diet meals for the month. The meals are designed to be frozen individually so that you can take them out of the freezer just as you need them.

Remember to label the meals, and it is probably a good idea to write down the calories of each one too. The less time you spend within the sight and smell of food, the more likely you are to stick to your diet. With lots of ready-prepared meals in the freezer you can cut down on the time you spend in the kitchen and shopping for ingredients. When you keep food in the refrigerator it is very easy to be tempted to nibble away at it every time you open the door. But frozen meals are far less tempting — and they'll take time to defrost anyway.

To make sure that foods do not dry out in the freezer they should be wrapped to exclude as much air as possible. You can wrap items such as sandwiches in freezer film or foil before putting them in a plastic bag. Save your empty cottage cheese or yogurt cartons for freezing individual desserts, pâtés, etc. Soups and liquids are best frozen in rigid containers and they need a little head space to expand.

It is a good idea to keep a record of what you freeze and what you use. This means that you can devise your dieting menus without opening your freezer to find out what meals you have available. Write down the date when you freeze, too, so that you can use up the oldest foods first. Sandwiches can usually be frozen for up to 2 months, and casseroles for about 4 months. Marinaded meats should be used up in 2-3 months. Spreads, pâtés and meat loaves should be used within a month, but soups will be perfectly fine for 3 months.

Devising your diet plan

If you are overweight you have been eating more calories than your body needs so it has stored the fat surplus to call upon in times of food shortage. And that shortage has never happened! When you reduce your calorie intake you will be drawing on that store. All men and most women will start using up that fat store if they eat no more than 1,500 calories a day. But to achieve a speedy weight loss, some women may have to cut down to 1,000 calories a day.

Use these guidelines. If you just have a few stubborn pounds to shift, then if you are a woman diet on 1,000 calories a day and if you are a man on 1,250 calories. With between 1st and 3st to lose you can add another 250 calories a day on to both those figures. When you start dieting with more than 3st to lose then start on 1,500 calories (1,750 calories if you are a man) and cut down on calories as you get nearer to your target.

Eating healthily while following a slimming diet is as important as eating fewer calories. Your daily calorie allowance must provide you with all the essential nutrients to keep your body functioning properly and, as you usually consume a little less food while slimming, it is especially important to make sure your diet is nutritionally sound. That means you must aim to eat from a wide range of foods to give variety and to supply the essential minerals, vitamins and protein. Include some wholegrain cereals, meat, fish and lower-fat dairy produce such as skimmed milk or reduced-fat cheeses. Eat plenty of vegetables and fruit. Keep confectionery, sugary soft drinks and alcohol to an absolute minimum.

Plan your menus in advance and make out a shopping list of all the things you will need so you don't suddenly find you are minus some vital ingredient.

Drink calorie-free beverages whenever you like, such as water, black coffee and tea, and stock up with low calorie fizzy or squash drinks. It is a good idea to include at least 275ml/½ pint skimmed milk (100 calories) in your daily allowance as milk is an excellent source of nutrients.

How to use this book

You can use a combination of freezer and microwave recipes in your diet plan. All the freezer recipes have instructions for reheating the meals either conventionally or in a microwave. Just choose the recipes you fancy, note their calories, then sit down and plan out some menus to add up to your total daily calorie aim. Remember to allow for vegetables when meals require these. There are breakfast, light meal and main meal suggestions, desserts and low calorie snacks. Good eating, good dieting!

QUICK START BREAKFASTS

Light fluffy scrambled eggs, porridge with no sticky pans to clean; even poached fruit is ready in minutes in a microwave. You can also use your microwave to make low-sugar, low calorie fruit spreads in small, manageable quantities. Any of the satisfying breakfasts in this chapter would also make excellent suppertime snacks.

HOT GRAPEFRUIT WITH SULTANAS

Serves 1/60 calories

½ medium grapefruit
10ml/2 level teaspoons
sultanas or raisins
5ml/1 level teaspoon
honey

1. Loosen the segments of the grapefruit and carefully lift out membranes between the segments.
2. Press the sultanas or raisins in the spaces between the segments.
3. Spread the honey on top.
4. Place in a serving dish and microwave on HIGH for 1¼ minutes.

WEST COAST FRUIT COMPOTE (See picture opposite page 32)

Serves 2/90 calories per portion

25g/1oz dried prunes
25g/1oz dried apricots
50ml/2floz orange juice
1 medium grapefruit
50g/2oz strawberries,
fresh or frozen, halved

1. Place dried fruit and orange juice in a small dish. Cover with a lid or pierced cling film and microwave on HIGH for 3½ minutes, stirring twice.
2. Leave to stand for 5 minutes. Peel and segment grapefruit: add to dried fruits with strawberries.

PORRIDGE & RAISINS (See picture opposite page 32)

Serves 1/140 calories

25g/1oz quick-cook
porridge oats
200ml/7floz water
15ml/1 level tablespoon
raisins

1. In a deep individual bowl mix together oats and water. Cover ¾ of bowl with cling film. Microwave on HIGH for 2 minutes, stirring after 1 minute.
2. Cover bowl completely and stand for 2 minutes.
3. Sprinkle with raisins and serve with skimmed milk if desired (add 5 calories per tablespoon).

POACHED EGG WITH SMOKED HADDOCK

Serves 1/190 calories

115g/4oz smoked haddock fillet
30ml/2 tablespoons skimmed milk
75ml/3floz water
1 egg, size 3

1. Place the fish in a dish with the milk. Cover with a lid or pierced cling film and microwave on HIGH for 2 minutes.
2. Cover with foil, shiny side down, and leave to stand while you poach the egg.
3. Place the water in a small, shallow dish. Microwave on HIGH until boiling — about 1½ minutes.
4. Break the egg into the water. Gently pierce the yolk with the point of a small, sharp knife. Cover with pierced cling film or a plate and microwave on HIGH for 45 seconds.
5. Leave to stand for 1-2 minutes.
6. Place the fish on a plate and serve the egg on top.

SCRAMBLED EGGS & CRISPBREADS (See picture opposite page 32)

Serves 1/220 calories

2 eggs, size 3
30ml/2 tablespoons skimmed milk
Salt and pepper
2 crispbreads

1. Beat together eggs, skimmed milk and seasoning in a jug.
2. Microwave on HIGH for 1½ minutes, stirring twice.
3. Serve with crispbreads.

BACON SANDWICH

Serves 1/265 calories

50g/2oz streaky bacon
2 slices wholemeal bread, 35g/1¼oz each
15ml/1 level tablespoon tomato ketchup

1. Place the bacon in a single layer between two double layers of kitchen paper. Microwave on HIGH for 1¾-2 minutes.
2. Pat dry with clean kitchen paper.
3. Spread bread with tomato ketchup and make into a sandwich with the bacon.

PRUNE YOGURT

Serves 1/130 calories

40g/1½oz prunes
75ml/3floz water
150ml/¼ pint low-fat
natural yogurt

1. Place the prunes in a bowl with the water. Cover with a lid or pierced cling film and microwave on HIGH for 4 minutes.
2. Leave to stand for 10 minutes.
3. Drain prunes and allow to cool.
4. Stone prunes and stir into the yogurt.

ORANGE AND LEMON CURD

715 calories per whole amount, 10 calories per 5ml/1 level teaspoon

40g/1½oz unsalted butter
60ml/4 tablespoons fresh
orange juice
10ml/2 level teaspoons
finely grated orange rind
45ml/3 tablespoons lemon
juice
10ml/2 level teaspoons
finely grated lemon rind
25g/1oz fructose
(fruit sugar)
3 eggs, size 2

1. Place the butter in a basin and microwave on HIGH until just melted.
2. Add the orange rind and juice, lemon rind and juice and fructose. Stir well. Cover with a lid or pierced cling film and microwave on HIGH for 30 seconds. Stir again.
3. Lightly beat the eggs but do not whisk them. Pour onto the hot mixture, stirring constantly.
4. Whisking lightly every 30 seconds, microwave on HIGH for 2½ minutes or until the mixture just coats the back of a spoon.
5. Continue to whisk lightly for another 5 minutes.
6. Pour into a warmed jam jar. Cover and leave to cool.
7. Store in the refrigerator and use within 2 weeks.

APPLE AND CINNAMON SPREAD

380 calories per whole amount, 5 calories per 5ml/1 level teaspoon

675g/1½lb Granny Smith apples
50ml/2floz apple juice
2.5ml/½ level teaspoon ground cinnamon
30ml/2 level tablespoons honey

1. Wash the apples, then slice them. (Do not peel or core.)
2. Place in a bowl with the apple juice. Cover with a lid or pierced cling film and microwave on HIGH for 12 minutes until really pulpy.
3. Rub pulp through sieve, discarding skin and pips.
4. Place pulp in a clean bowl and stir in the cinnamon and honey. Microwave, uncovered, on HIGH until thick and creamy, stirring every 3 minutes. The time will vary from batch to batch.
5. Pour into a warmed jam jar and cover. Leave to cool.
6. Store in the refrigerator and use within 2 weeks.

PLUM SPREAD

325 calories per whole amount, 5 calories per 5ml/1 level teaspoon

45ml/3 tablespoons water
10ml/2 level teaspoons powdered gelatine
350g/12oz dessert plums, stoned and diced
45ml/3 tablespoons concentrated apple juice
30ml/2 level tablespoons fructose (fruit sugar)

1. Place the water in a small basin and sprinkle on the gelatine. Leave to soak.
2. Place plums in a bowl with the concentrated apple juice. Microwave, uncovered, on HIGH for 7 minutes, stirring every 2½ minutes.
3. Add the soaked gelatine and fructose and stir until completely dissolved.
4. Pour into a warmed jam jar and cover. Leave to cool.
5. Store in the refrigerator and use within 2 weeks.

BACON, MUSHROOM & TOMATO (See picture opposite page 32)

Serves 1/120 calories

2 rashers streaky bacon
50g/2oz button
mushrooms
10ml/2 teaspoons water
1 tomato, halved

1. Remove rind from bacon.
2. Place mushrooms and water in a dish, cover with a lid or pierced cling film. Microwave on HIGH for 1 minute. Leave to stand.
3. Place bacon between two double layers of kitchen paper on a plate. Microwave on HIGH for 1 minute. Remove top layer of paper. Place tomato on plate with bacon, cover and microwave on HIGH for 1 minute.

BLACKBERRY SPREAD

315 calories per whole amount, 5 calories per 5ml/1 level teaspoon

30ml/2 tablespoons water
7.5ml/1½ level teaspoons
powdered gelatine
225g/8oz blackberries,
fresh or frozen
75ml/5 tablespoons
concentrated apple juice
30ml/2 level tablespoons
fructose (fruit sugar)

1. Place the water in a small basin and sprinkle on the gelatine. Leave to soak.
2. Meanwhile place the frozen blackberries in a large bowl and microwave, uncovered, on HIGH for 3 minutes to thaw. Stir when half thawed.
3. Add the concentrated apple juice to the fresh or thawed blackberries and microwave, uncovered, on HIGH for 8 minutes, stirring twice.
4. Add the gelatine and fructose and stir until completely dissolved.
5. Pour into a warmed jam jar. Cover and leave to cool.
6. Store in the refrigerator and use within 2 weeks.

RASPBERRY AND NECTARINE SPREAD

340 calories per whole amount, 5 calories per 5ml/1 level teaspoon

45ml/3 tablespoons water
10ml/2 level teaspoons
powdered gelatine
225g/8oz raspberries,
fresh or frozen
115g/4oz nectarine flesh,
chopped (weighed without
skin and stones)
60ml/4 tablespoons
concentrated apple juice
30ml/2 level tablespoons
fructose (fruit sugar)

1. Place the water in a small basin and sprinkle on the gelatine. Leave to soak.
2. Place the frozen raspberries in a bowl and microwave, uncovered, on HIGH for 3 minutes to thaw. Stir when half thawed.
3. Add the concentrated apple juice to the nectarine flesh and the fresh or thawed raspberries. Microwave, uncovered, on HIGH for 10 minutes, stirring every 3 minutes.
4. Add the soaked gelatine and fructose. Stir until completely dissolved.
5. Pour into a warmed jam jar and cover. Leave to cool.
6. Store in the refrigerator and use within 2 weeks.

APRICOT SPREAD

565 calories per whole amount, 10 calories per 5ml/1 level teaspoon

175g/6oz dried apricots,
chopped
15ml/1 level tablespoon
finely grated orange rind
90ml/6 tablespoons
orange juice
60ml/4 tablespoons water
75ml/5 tablespoons
concentrated apple juice
15ml/1 level tablespoon
honey

1. Place all the ingredients in a bowl.
2. Cover with a lid or pierced cling film and microwave on HIGH for 12 minutes, stirring every 3 minutes.
3. Purée in a blender or food processor.
4. Pour into a warmed jam jar. Cover and leave to cool.
5. Store in the refrigerator and use within 2 weeks.

SCRAMBLED EGG WITH HAM AND MUSHROOMS

Serves 1/195 calories

25g/1oz button mushrooms, thinly sliced
15ml/1 tablespoon skimmed milk
25g/1oz lean cooked ham
1 egg, size 3
Pepper
1 slice wholemeal bread, 35g/1¼ oz

1. Place the mushrooms in a small bowl with the milk. Cover with a lid or pierced cling film and microwave on HIGH for 1¼ minutes.
2. Drain and reserve 15ml/1 tablespoon liquid.
3. Discard all visible fat from the ham and chop the lean.
4. Lightly beat the egg with the reserved liquid from the mushrooms. Season with pepper. Microwave, uncovered, on HIGH for 30 seconds.
5. Whisk, then stir in mushrooms and ham. Cook on HIGH for a further 15-30 seconds or until lightly set.
6. Leave to stand for 1 minute.
7. While the egg is cooking, toast the bread under the grill or in a toaster. Serve the egg mixture on top.

MICROWAVE LIGHT MEALS

Even if you eat lunch on your own, it pays never to just grab a snack on the wing. That lump of Cheddar cheese and couple of cream crackers spread with butter can easily add up to around 400 calories. Here you'll find light meals, such as soups, hot rolls, filled pitta breads, omelets and baked potatoes which can be made just for one. They are quick and easy to prepare, tasty and low calorie too. You'll also find some light meals that are well worth sharing.

PEA SOUP

Serves 1/125 calories

½ small onion, chopped
50g/2oz potato, peeled
weight, diced
Pinch dried mixed herbs
Pinch sugar
175ml/6floz boiling water
50g/2oz frozen peas
½ chicken stock cube
15ml/1 level tablespoon
skimmed milk powder

1. Place the onion, potato, herbs, sugar and 30ml/2 tablespoons boiling water in a bowl. Cover with a lid or pierced cling film and microwave on HIGH for 2 minutes.
2. Add the peas. Cover again and microwave on HIGH for 2 minutes.
3. Dissolve the stock cube in remaining boiling water and leave to cool for a few moments. Add the skimmed milk powder.
4. Place in a blender or food processor with the vegetables and purée until smooth.
5. Pour into a serving bowl and reheat in the microwave on HIGH for 1 minute.

Serving Suggestion:
On its own makes a filling low calorie snack. Serve with a 45g/1¾oz wholemeal roll and you have a good light meal for 250 calories.

MUSHROOM SOUP

Serves 1/75 calories

½ small onion, chopped
½ bay leaf
50g/2oz mushrooms,
chopped
Small pinch dried mixed
herbs
¼ chicken stock cube,
crumbled
200ml/7floz boiling water
10ml/2 level teaspoons
cornflour
30ml/2 level tablespoons
skimmed milk powder
45ml/3 tablespoons cold
water
Salt and pepper

1. Place the onion, bay leaf, mushrooms, herbs, crumbled stock cube and boiling water in a large bowl. Cover with a lid or pierced cling film and microwave on HIGH for 3½ minutes, stirring every 2 minutes. Discard the bay leaf.
2. Purée in a blender or food processor. Return to the bowl.
3. Mix the cornflour, skimmed milk powder and cold water until smooth. Stir into the bowl. Microwave on HIGH until boiling and thickened — about 3½ minutes — stirring every 30 seconds. Season to taste and serve.

Serving Suggestion:
Makes a very low calorie starter for a meal — even if you add a wholemeal roll your snack's total will only be 200 calories.

WATERCRESS SOUP WITH CROUTONS (See picture opposite page 33)

Serves 1/165 calories

1 small onion, chopped
30ml/2 tablespoons water
40g/1½oz watercress, trimmed and stalks discarded
½ chicken stock cube
175ml/6floz hot water
30ml/2 level tablespoons dry instant potato powder
15ml/1 level tablespoon dried skimmed milk
Salt and pepper
15g/½oz wholemeal bread, toasted

1. Place onion in a deep dish with water, cover with a lid or pierced cling film and microwave on HIGH for 2 minutes.
2. Place watercress in bowl with onions.
3. Dissolve stock cube in hot water and add to watercress. Cover and microwave on HIGH for 3 minutes.
4. Purée in a blender or food processor with instant potato powder and skimmed milk powder.
5. Pour back into bowl. Season. Reheat on HIGH for 1 minute. Cube toast and sprinkle over soup.

Serving Suggestion:
Ideal as a low calorie late night snack which is nicely filling.

CELERY SOUP WITH BLUE CHEESE

Serves 1/145 calories

50g/2oz celery, chopped
25g/1oz onion, chopped
50g/2oz potato, peeled weight, diced
175ml/6floz boiling water
½ chicken stock cube
15ml/1 level tablespoon skimmed milk powder
15g/½oz Stilton or Danish Blue cheese

1. Place the celery, onion and potato in a bowl with 30ml/2 tablespoons boiling water. Cover with a lid or pierced cling film and microwave on HIGH for 4 minutes.
2. Dissolve the stock cube in the remaining boiling water. Leave to cool slightly for 1 minute, then stir in the skimmed milk powder.
3. Pour into a blender or food processor and add the vegetables. Purée until smooth.
4. Pour into a soup bowl and reheat in the microwave on HIGH for 1 minute. Crumble the cheese on top and serve.

Serving Suggestion:
On its own as a snack or with a wholemeal roll or bread. A medium-slice from a wholemeal long loaf costs 70 calories, which would bring your light meal's total up to 215 calories.

CRISPY TOPPED VEGETABLE MEDLEY (See picture opposite page 33)

Serves 1/310 calories

140g/4.9oz can condensed
cream of celery soup
45ml/3 tablespoons
skimmed milk
225g/8oz country mix
vegetables, frozen
15g/½oz fresh wholemeal
breadcrumbs
15ml/1 level tablespoon
Parmesan cheese

1. Stir the soup and skimmed milk together in a small dish and add the frozen vegetables.
2. Cover with a lid or pierced cling film and microwave on HIGH for 7 minutes.
3. Mix together breadcrumbs and Parmesan cheese. Sprinkle over vegetables and place under a grill to brown the breadcrumbs.

Serving Suggestion:
A complete meal on its own. Or if you wish eat with a couple of crispbreads.

SPINACH AND BACON CUSTARD

Serves 1/230 calories

115g/4oz spinach, frozen,
chopped
1 rasher streaky bacon,
25g/1oz
1 spring onion, trimmed
and thinly sliced
115ml/4floz skimmed milk
1 egg, size 3
Salt and pepper
15ml/1 level tablespoon
grated Parmesan cheese

1. Thaw spinach in the microwave on DEFROST for 5 minutes. Place in a sieve and press lightly to drain off all excess moisture.
2. Place bacon between two double layers of kitchen paper. Microwave on HIGH for 1¼-1½ minutes until crisp. Pat dry with clean paper. Break into small pieces.
3. Measure the milk into a measuring jug. Heat on HIGH for 1 minute but do not allow to boil.
4. Beat egg lightly and whisk into the milk. Stir in spinach, bacon and spring onion. Season.
5. Pour into a dish about 15cm/ 6 inches in diameter. Sprinkle Parmesan cheese on top. Stand dish in a larger dish and pour in enough boiling water to come up as far as the custard.
6. Microwave on HIGH for 4-5 minutes or until only just set in the middle. Leave to stand for 5 minutes.

Serving Suggestion:
Makes a tasty light meal to which you only need to add a crispbread or two.

CHEESE SOUFFLÉ

Serves 4/230 calories per portion

**5ml/1 level teaspoon plus
25g/1oz low-fat spread
175ml/6floz skimmed milk
1 bay leaf
1 slice onion
25g/1oz cornflour
50g/2oz mature Cheddar
cheese, grated
25g/1oz Parmesan cheese
(preferably from a block),
grated
Salt and pepper
1.25ml/¼ level teaspoon
dry mustard
3 eggs, size 2, separated**

1. Grease a 1.4 litre/2½ pint soufflé dish with 5ml/1 level teaspoon low-fat spread.
2. Place 150ml/¼ pint milk in a bowl with the bay leaf and onion. Microwave on HIGH for 2 minutes. Cover and leave to stand for 20 minutes. Discard the bay leaf and onion.
3. Blend the cornflour with the remaining milk and add to the hot milk. Stir well. Add the 25g/1oz low-fat spread and microwave on HIGH until boiling and thickened, whisking every 30 seconds.
4. Stir the cheeses into the sauce. Season with salt, pepper and mustard.
5. Beat the egg yolks into the sauce. Whisk the whites until stiff and fold in gently. Turn into the dish.
6. Microwave on DEFROST for 15 minutes. Serve immediately.

Serving Suggestion:
This soufflé won't keep, so only serve it when there are four people to share. By the way, if you can't buy a piece of Parmesan (the ready grated sort doesn't have as good a flavour) replace it with an extra 25g/1oz mature Cheddar. Serve the soufflé with a crisp green salad.

CHEESE AND VEGETABLE PITTA

Serves 1/315 calories

**50g/2oz courgettes, thinly
sliced
25g/1oz red or green
pepper, deseeded and
diced
1 medium tomato,
chopped
Small pinch dried mixed
herbs
15ml/1 level tablespoon
tomato ketchup
25g/1oz Cotswold cheese
or Double Gloucester with
chives, grated
1 wholemeal pitta bread**

1. Place the courgettes and pepper in a small dish. Cover with a lid or pierced cling film and microwave on HIGH for 1 minute. Add the tomato, herbs, tomato ketchup and cheese.
2. Cut the pitta bread in half and slide a knife between the layers to form 2 pockets.
3. Fill with vegetable mixture.
4. Place pitta on a plate on kitchen paper. Microwave on HIGH for 1 minute. Serve immediately.

Serving Suggestion:
Although you could serve this pitta with a green salad, it is filled with lots of vegetables and is a complete meal on its own.

CHOWDER

Serves 2/165 calories per portion

50g/2oz potato, peeled weight, diced
1 spring onion, leaves discarded, thinly sliced
325ml/11floz boiling water
¼ fish stock cube
75g/3oz smoked haddock fillet
75g/3oz canned sweetcorn, drained
50g/2oz prawns
15ml/1 level tablespoon skimmed milk powder
20ml/4 level teaspoons cornflour
30ml/2 tablespoons cold water
Pepper

1. Place the potato and onion in a bowl with 30ml/2 tablespoons boiling water and cover with a lid or pierced cling film. Microwave on HIGH for 3 minutes.
2. Dissolve the fish stock cube in 150ml/¼ pint boiling water and add to the potato and onion. Place the fish and sweetcorn on top. Cover and microwave on HIGH for 2 minutes or until fish flakes easily.
3. Lift out the fish and discard skin and bones. Return fish to the bowl with the prawns and an extra 150ml/¼ pint boiling water.
4. Blend the skimmed milk powder and cornflour with the cold water and then stir into the dish. Microwave on HIGH until boiling and thickened — about 2 minutes — stirring well every 30 seconds. Season with pepper.

Serving Suggestion:
This substantial soup makes a filling light meal if served with wholemeal bread or roll. If you don't intend to share your meal, the second portion will keep in the refrigerator until the next day.

POPPADOM WITH SPICY EGGS

Serves 1/290 calories

1 poppadom
5ml/1 level teaspoon butter
1.25ml/¼ level teaspoon curry powder
1 spring onion, leaves discarded, thinly sliced
25g/1oz green pepper, deseeded and diced
2 eggs, size 3
30ml/2 tablespoons skimmed milk
Salt and pepper

1. Place the poppadom in a cereal bowl and microwave, uncovered, on HIGH for 30 seconds.
2. Place the butter, curry powder, spring onion and green pepper in a bowl. Cover with a lid or pierced cling film and microwave on HIGH for 1 minute. Stir, cover again, and cook on HIGH for a further minute.
3. Lightly beat the eggs and milk together. Season with salt and pepper and add to the vegetables.
4. Microwave on HIGH for 1½ minutes, whisking every 30 seconds, until lightly set. Pile onto the poppadom and serve.

Serving Suggestion:
Eat with crunchy raw vegetable sticks. Try carrots, celery and red or green peppers. You'll probably not munch your way through more than 30 calories' worth.

TUNA PITTA

Serves 1/335 calories

5ml/1 level teaspoon
butter
50g/2oz button
mushrooms, sliced
2.5ml/½ level teaspoon
cornflour
30ml/2 tablespoons milk
50g/2oz tuna, canned in
brine, drained and flaked
50g/2oz canned sweetcorn
with peppers, drained
Pepper
1 wholemeal pitta bread

1. Microwave the butter in a bowl on HIGH until melted — about 20 seconds.
2. Add the mushrooms and stir until they are well coated. Cover with a lid or pierced cling film and microwave on HIGH for 1¼ minutes.
3. Mix the cornflour with the milk until smooth and stir into the bowl. Microwave on HIGH for 1½ minutes, stirring every 30 seconds.
4. Stir in the tuna and sweetcorn with peppers. Season with pepper.
5. Cut the pitta bread in half and slide a knife between the layers to make 2 pockets. Fill with the tuna mixture.
6. Place pitta on a plate on a piece of kitchen paper and microwave on HIGH for 1 minute.

Serving Suggestion:
A meal on its own or you can add a little green salad.

CRAB SOUFFLÉ

Serves 4/210 calories per portion

5ml/1 level teaspoon plus
25g/1oz low-fat spread
175ml/6floz skimmed milk
25g/1oz cornflour
200g/7oz crab meat (brown
and white mixed), flaked
15ml/1 level tablespoon
tomato ketchup
2.5ml/½ level teaspoon
paprika
3 eggs, size 2, separated
Salt and pepper
15ml/1 level tablespoon
ready-grated Parmesan
cheese

1. Grease a 1.4 litre/2½ pint soufflé dish with 5ml/1 level teaspoon low-fat spread.
2. In a bowl mix a little of the milk with the cornflour until smooth. Add the remaining milk and 25g/1oz low-fat spread. Microwave on HIGH until boiling and thickened — about 2½ minutes — whisking every 30 seconds.
3. Stir in the crab meat, tomato ketchup and paprika. Add the egg yolks and season.
4. Whisk the egg whites until stiff and fold in gently. Turn into the dish and sprinkle with Parmesan cheese. Microwave on DEFROST for 15-18 minutes or until the centre of the top is just cooked. Serve immediately.

Serving Suggestion:
Serve with a green salad, peas or broccoli. You can pile up your plate with salad greens and they are unlikely to cost you more than 25 calories. Add a tablespoon of oil-free French dressing if you wish (5 calories) or try a low calorie seafood dressing (sometimes called tomato dressing for seafoods and salads) which costs 20 calories per 15ml/1 level tablespoon.

PICCALILLI 'N' PINEAPPLE PITTA PIZZA
(See picture opposite page 33)

Serves 1/325 calories

1 wholemeal pitta bread
15ml/1 level tablespoon piccalilli
1 tomato, sliced
1 ring pineapple canned in natural juice, chopped
25g/1oz mature Cheddar cheese, grated
1 black olive, stoned and sliced into rings
Chopped parsley

1. Spread pitta bread with piccalilli.
2. Place the tomato and pineapple on pitta bread. Sprinkle with cheese.
3. Place on plate on kitchen paper and microwave on HIGH for 1½ minutes.
4. Arrange olive on pizza and sprinkle with parsley before serving.

Serving Suggestion:
Just add a little shredded lettuce.

CURRIED EGG PITTA BREAD

Serves 1/330 calories

1 spring onion, leaves discarded, thinly sliced
2.5ml/½ teaspoon oil
1.25ml/¼ level teaspoon curry powder
1 tomato, chopped
2.5ml/½ level teaspoon cornflour
15ml/1 tablespoon water
15ml/1 level tablespoon mango chutney
Salt and pepper
1 egg, size 3, hard boiled and chopped
1 wholemeal pitta bread

1. Mix together the spring onion, oil and curry powder. Cover with a lid or pierced cling film and microwave on HIGH for 30 seconds.
2. Stir in the tomato. Cover and microwave on HIGH for 30 seconds.
3. Mix cornflour with water until smooth. Stir into curry mixture with mango chutney. Cover and microwave on HIGH for 1½ minutes, stirring every 30 seconds. Season with salt and pepper. Stir in the egg.
4. Cut the pitta in half and slide a knife between the layers to make 2 pockets. Fill with the egg mixture.
5. Place on a piece of kitchen paper on a plate and microwave on HIGH for 1 minute, uncovered.

Serving Suggestion:
A complete meal on its own, but eat with a green salad if you wish.

CHEESE AND TOMATO OMELET

Serves 1/235 calories

2 eggs, size 3
15ml/1 tablespoon water
Pepper
15g/½oz mature Cheddar
cheese, grated
1.25ml/¼ level teaspoon
low-fat spread
1 tomato, sliced
1 spring onion, leaves
discarded, sliced

1. Beat the eggs and water together and season with pepper. Add the cheese.
2. Grease a shallow 15cm/6 inch or 18cm/7 inch round dish with low-fat spread. Microwave on HIGH for 10 seconds.
3. Pour in the eggs and microwave on HIGH for 30 seconds. Draw the cooked mixture towards the centre of the dish and tilt so that the raw mixture goes underneath.
4. Microwave on HIGH for a further 30 seconds. Lift the edges and tilt the dish again.
5. Arrange the tomato and onion on top. Return to the microwave for a further 1-2 minutes.

Serving Suggestion:
A 115g/4oz helping of whole green beans will add just 40 calories to your meal's total. Or serve with a salad.

PARSLEY AND HAM OMELET

Serves 1/195 calories

2 eggs, size 3
15ml/1 tablespoon water
5ml/1 level teaspoon
parsley, chopped
Pepper
1.25ml/¼ level teaspoon
low-fat spread
25g/1oz lean cooked ham,
trimmed of fat and
chopped

1. Beat together the eggs, water and parsley until evenly mixed. Season with pepper.
2. Grease a 15cm/6 inch or 18cm/7 inch shallow dish with the low-fat spread. Microwave on HIGH for 10 seconds.
3. Pour in the eggs and microwave on HIGH for 30 seconds. Draw the cooked mixture to the centre. Tilt the dish and lift the edges so that the raw mixture goes underneath.
4. Microwave on HIGH for a further 30 seconds. Lift the edges and tilt the dish again.
5. Sprinkle the ham on top. Microwave on HIGH for 1½ minutes or until just cooked. Serve immediately.

Serving Suggestion:
Try with a tomato salad — 2 tomatoes thinly sliced, sprinkled with a little parsley if you wish, and topped with a 15ml/1 tablespoon wine vinegar. Costs an extra 25 calories.

SARDINE MUFFIN PIZZA

Serves 2/165 calories per portion

**1 wholemeal muffin, 70g/2½oz
1 tomato, sliced
1 spring onion, trimmed and sliced
50g/2oz sardines canned in tomato sauce, drained
Pinch dried basil or mixed herbs
25g/1oz Edam cheese, grated**

1. Split the muffin and place, cut side up, on a piece of kitchen paper on a plate. Arrange the tomato on top.
2. Mix the spring onion with the sardines and herbs. Spread over the tomato. Top with the cheese.
3. Microwave, uncovered, on HIGH for 2 minutes.

Serving Suggestion:
Wholemeal muffins make a filling pizza base and this is a good lunchtime recipe to share with a dieting friend. Add a green salad if you wish.

HAM AND SPINACH ROLLS

Serves 1/205 calories

**115g/4oz spinach, frozen, chopped
25g/1oz curd cheese
Salt and pepper
3 slices cooked ham, 25g/1oz each, trimmed of fat
115ml/4floz tomato juice
Dash Worcestershire sauce
5ml/1 level teaspoon cornflour
Pinch dried basil or mixed herbs**

1. Thaw spinach in the microwave on DEFROST for 5 minutes. Place in a sieve and press lightly to drain off all excess moisture.
2. Mix spinach with curd cheese and season with salt and pepper.
3. Spread mixture on the ham slices and roll up. Place in a single dish, not quite touching, in a shallow dish.
4. Blend tomato juice, Worcestershire sauce and cornflour together in a bowl. Add the basil or mixed herbs. Microwave on HIGH until boiling, stirring every 30 seconds.
5. Pour the hot sauce over the ham rolls. Microwave on HIGH for 3 minutes.

Serving Suggestion:
Good with broccoli, microwaved or steamed, count 30 calories for a 115g/4oz portion weighed raw.

CRUMPET SAUSAGE PIZZA

Serves 1/170 calories

1 crumpet
5ml/1 level teaspoon tomato ketchup
1 small tomato or ½ medium tomato, sliced
Pinch dried basil
15g/½oz garlic sausage, sliced
15g/½oz Edam cheese, grated
1 stuffed olive, sliced

1. Place on a piece of kitchen paper on a plate and put the crumpet on top.
2. Spread crumpet with tomato ketchup, then arrange the tomato on top. Sprinkle with basil. Top with the garlic sausage, grated cheese and olive.
3. Microwave on HIGH for 1 minute.

Serving Suggestion:
This pizza is low enough in calories for you to afford to eat it as a snack. Although you only use a little garlic sausage (weigh carefully as calories are high) it is satisfyingly strong flavoured. Two crumpet pizzas would make a substantial main meal served with a little lettuce.

'CREAMED' MUSHROOMS ON TOAST

Serves 1/170 calories

115g/4oz small button mushrooms
75ml/3floz skimmed milk
½ bay leaf
15ml/1 level tablespoon cornflour
Salt and pepper
40g/1½oz slice wholemeal bread, toasted

1. Place the mushrooms, 50ml/2floz milk and bay leaf in a dish. Cover with a lid or pierced cling film and microwave on HIGH for 3 minutes.
2. Mix the cornflour with remaining milk until smooth and stir into the dish.
3. Microwave on HIGH until boiling and thickened — about 1 minute — stirring every 30 seconds.
4. Discard bay leaf. Season with salt and pepper and serve on the toast.

Serving Suggestion:
Makes an ideal low calorie suppertime snack.

BAKED POTATO WITH BEANS

Serves 1/265 calories

1 potato, 225g/8oz,
scrubbed and pricked
150g/5.3oz can baked
beans in tomato sauce

1. Place the potato on a double thickness of kitchen paper and microwave on HIGH for 3½ minutes.
2. Turn over and reposition and microwave on HIGH for a further 3½ minutes. Leave to stand for 3 minutes.
3. If not cooked through, microwave for a further 1 minute.
4. Place the baked beans in a small dish and cover with a lid or pierced cling film. Microwave on HIGH for 1 minute.
5. Cut the potato in half and spoon the baked beans on top.

Serving Suggestion:
A very filling meal on its own. If you wish you could add a tomato, which will cost an extra 12 calories.

SMOKY MACKEREL POTATO (See picture opposite page 33)

Serves 1/310 calories

200g/7oz potato
15ml/1 level tablespoon
horseradish sauce
15ml/1 tablespoon
skimmed milk
50g/2oz smoked mackerel,
flaked
1 spring onion, chopped

1. Scrub potato and pierce with a fork. Place on a double piece of kitchen towel and microwave on HIGH for 3 minutes.
2. Turn over and reposition. Cook for a further 3 minutes. Leave to stand for 3 minutes.
3. Cut open the potato and scoop out the flesh. Mash potato with horseradish sauce and skimmed milk.
4. Mix smoked mackerel and spring onion with mashed potato. Spoon back into potato skins and microwave on HIGH for 1 minute.

Serving Suggestion:
Add a mixed green salad of lettuce, cucumber and cress.

BAKED POTATO WITH PRAWNS (See cover picture)

Serves 1/270 calories

225g/8oz potato
25g/1oz green pepper
50g/2oz skimmed milk
soft cheese
40g/1½oz prawns, peeled

1. Place the potato on a double thickness of kitchen paper and microwave on HIGH for 3½ minutes.
2. Turn over and reposition. Cook for a further 3½ minutes. Leave to stand for 3 minutes.
3. Dice pepper and mix with sklimmed milk soft cheese.
4. Cut a cross in the top of the potato and squeeze gently to open. Top with soft cheese, pepper and prawns.

Serving Suggestion:
Place on a bed of shredded iceberg lettuce and add cucumber slices. Calories for these greens are so low they are scarcely worth counting.

BAKED POTATO WITH CHEESE

Serves 1/290 calories

1 potato, 200g/7oz, scrubbed and pricked
25g/1oz fat-reduced hard cheese, grated
50g/2oz cottage cheese with chives and onion
15ml/1 tablespoon skimmed milk
Salt and pepper

1. Place the potato on a double thickness of kitchen paper and microwave on HIGH for 3 minutes.
2. Turn over and reposition. Cook for a further 3 minutes. Leave to stand for 3 minutes.
3. Test and if not cooked through, microwave for a further 1 minute.
4. Cut in half and carefully scoop out the flesh, leaving the skin intact. Mash potato flesh with the hard cheese, cottage cheese and milk. Season with salt and pepper.
5. Pile back into the potato skins and place on kitchen paper. Microwave on HIGH for 2 minutes to reheat.

Serving Suggestion:
A complete meal on its own or serve with tomato slices.

MAIN MEALS
IN MINUTES

Poultry and fish are extra succulent cooked in a microwave and other lean and tender cuts of meat and offal are good too. In this chapter you'll find ideas for easy main meals and some extra-special recipes for when you feel like indulging yourself. Many of the recipes serve one, but there are also meals that make two and four servings. If you do decide to double up any of the recipes for extra servings, remember that the microwave times will need to be extended.

BARBECUED CHICKEN

Serves 1/265 calories

2 chicken thighs, 115g/4oz
each
15ml/1 level tablespoon
tomato ketchup
15ml/1 level tablespoon
tomato relish
15ml/ 1 level tablespoon
brown sauce
5ml/1 level teaspoon soft
brown sugar
5ml/1 teaspoon wine
vinegar
2.5ml/½ teaspoon
Worcestershire sauce
2.5ml/½ teaspoon Soy
sauce

1. Place chicken thighs in a dish.
Cover and microwave on HIGH for
1½ minutes.
2. Turn chicken over and
rearrange. Cook on HIGH for a
further 1½ minutes.
3. Discard the skin and drain off
any fat that has cooked out.
4. Place all the remaining
ingredients in a jug and mix well.
Cover and microwave on HIGH for
1 minute.
5. Pour over the chicken thighs.
Cover and microwave on HIGH for
3½ minutes.

Serving Suggestion:
**A lot of fatty calories lurk in
the skin of chicken so don't be
tempted to serve these joints
unskinned. Serve with a jacket
baked potato, 200g/7oz raw
weight, for a really substantial
meal costing 420 calories in
total.**

CHICKEN AND SWEETCORN PILAFF

Serves 2/385 calories per portion

75g/3oz onion, chopped
15ml/1 tablespoon cold
water
5ml/1 level teaspoon
butter
50g/2oz red or green
pepper, deseeded and
diced
1.25ml/¼ level teaspoon
mixed dried herbs
15ml/1 level tablespoon
tomato purée
115g/4oz long-grain white
rice
1 chicken stock cube
275ml/½ pint boiling
water
115g/4oz cooked chicken
115g/4oz canned
sweetcorn, drained

1. Place the onion in a casserole-
size dish with the water and butter.
Cover with a lid or pierced cling
film and microwave on HIGH for 3
minutes. Stir.
2. Add pepper to the onion, cover
and microwave on HIGH for 1
minute.
3. Stir in the herbs, tomato purée
and rice.
4. Dissolve the stock cube in the
boiling water, then add to the rice.
Cover and cook on HIGH for 12
minutes. Cover with foil, shiny side
down, and leave to stand for 5
minutes.
5. Discard the skin from the
chicken and cut the meat into
small pieces. Stir into the pilaff
with the sweetcorn. Cover and
microwave on HIGH for 2 minutes.

Serving Suggestion:
**This dish serves two, but you
could save one portion in the
refrigerator for the next day.
Serve with a mixed green salad
of lettuce, cucumber, cress
plus 15ml/1 tablespoon oil-free
French dressing and count 30
extra calories.**

PERSIAN STUFFED CHICKEN (See picture opposite page 65)

Serves 1/230 calories

115g/4oz boned chicken breast, skin removed
½ small onion, chopped
15ml/1 tablespoon water
3 ready-to-eat dried apricots, chopped
15ml/1 level tablespoon raisins
60ml/4 level tablespoons fresh white breadcrumbs

1. Place the chicken between two pieces of greaseproof paper and beat until almost double in size.
2. Place onion and water in a dish. Cover with a lid or pierced cling film and microwave on HIGH for 2 minutes.
3. Mix apricots with drained onions, raisins and breadcrumbs. Spread over chicken breast. Fold in the ends and roll up. Secure with 2 wooden cocktail sticks.
4. Place in a dish, cover and microwave on HIGH for 3 minutes.
5. Slice chicken breast and serve.

Serving Suggestion:
Add 115g/4oz broccoli, boiled, and your calorie total is still only 260 calories.

TURKEY IN SWEETCORN SAUCE

Serves 1/300 calories

150g/5oz turkey breast fillet
75ml/3floz boiling water
¼ chicken stock cube
Pinch dried thyme
30ml/2 level tablespoons powdered skimmed milk
5ml/1 level teaspoon cornflour
25g/1oz lean cooked ham, trimmed of fat
75g/3oz canned sweetcorn and peppers, drained
Salt and pepper

1. Cut turkey into five even-sized pieces and place in a small casserole dish.
2. Dissolve stock cube in boiling water.
3. Add 30ml/2 tablespoons stock and the thyme to turkey. Cover with a lid or pierced cling film. Cook on HIGH for 5 minutes, stirring after 3 minutes. Remove turkey and cover with foil to keep warm.
4. Blend skimmed milk powder and cornflour with the cold stock until smooth. Add to the juices in the casserole dish. Cook on HIGH for 1 minute, stirring briskly every 20 seconds until boiling and thickened.
5. Cut the ham into small strips. Add to the sauce with the sweetcorn and turkey. Cover and heat on HIGH for 1 minute. Season and serve.

Serving Suggestion:
Add a portion of green beans and count 5 calories for each boiled or microwaved 25g/1oz.

4 5 6
7 8 9
COOK
CONTROL 0 TIME

CLEAR START STOP

COOK CONTROL
10 Low Softening Cream Cheese
20 Warm Warming Food
30 Defrost Thawing Food
40 Inable Slow Cooking Dishes
50 Simmer Cooking Stews & Soups
60 Bake Cakes & Desserts
70 Roast Cooking Roasts, Ham
80 Reheat Reheating Food
90 Sauté Sautéing Vegetables
100 High Poultry, Fruit, Vegetables

**UICK START
CROWAVE
REAKFASTS**

con, Mushroom
d Tomato;
rambled Eggs and
spbreads;
rridge and Raisins;
st Coast Fruit
mpote

MICROWAVE LIGHT MEALS
Watercress Soup with Croutons;
Piccalilli 'n' Pineapple Pitta Pizza;
Smoky Mackerel Potato; Crispy
Topped Vegetable Medley

CHICKEN WITH MUSHROOM SAUCE

Serves 1/235 calories

150g/5oz skinless chicken
breast fillet
50g/2oz button
mushrooms, sliced
1 spring onion, trimmed
and sliced
Pinch dried thyme or
1.25ml/¼ level teaspoon
chopped fresh thyme
¼ chicken stock cube
5ml/1 level teaspoon
cornflour
30ml/2 level tablespoons
powdered skimmed milk
Salt and pepper

1. Place the chicken in a dish and cover with a lid or pierced cling film. Microwave on HIGH for 1½ minutes.
2. Turn the chicken over, cover again and microwave on HIGH for another 1½ minutes.
3. Place the mushrooms and the spring onion around the chicken and sprinkle with thyme.
4. Add 30ml/2 tablespoons water. Cover dish and microwave on HIGH for a further 2 minutes. Leave to stand for 2 minutes, then check that the chicken is cooked through. The exact cooking time will vary slightly depending on the thickness of the chicken. If it is not quite cooked remove the mushrooms and onion and set aside, then cover the chicken again and microwave on HIGH for 1 minute.
5. Drain the liquid into a measuring jug and stir in the stock cube until dissolved. Make up to 75ml/3floz with cold water.
6. Add the cornflour and powdered skimmed milk and mix until smooth. Microwave on HIGH until boiling and thickened, stirring briskly every 30 seconds.
7. Season to taste with salt and pepper. Pour over the chicken and vegetables. Microwave on HIGH for 30 seconds to heat through.

Serving Suggestion:
New potatoes microwaved or boiled in their skins and boiled sliced carrots would make excellent accompaniments. Count 85 calories for 115g/4oz potatoes weighed raw and peeled and 25 calories for the same amount of carrots.

VEAL CORDON BLEU

Serves 1/190 calories

75g/3oz veal escalope
15g/½oz lean cooked ham, trimmed of all fat
15g/½oz Edam cheese, thinly sliced
2.5ml/½ teaspoon oil
2.5ml/½ level teaspoon butter

1. Put the veal escalope between sheets of greaseproof paper and batter with a rolling pin until thin and about twice its size. Place the ham on half of the veal, folding it if necessary so that the ham does not overlap the edges. Place the cheese on top. Fold the other half of the veal over the ham and cheese and press the edges together. Secure with a wooden cocktail stick.
2. Place butter and oil in a small dish and microwave on HIGH until melted — about 20 seconds.
3. Add the veal parcel to the dish and brush all over with the fat. Microwave on HIGH for 2 minutes.
4. Turn over and reposition. Microwave on HIGH for 2 minutes. Leave to stand for 3 minutes.

Serving Suggestion:
Delicious with mangetout — 12 calories per 28g/1oz weighed frozen or boiled — and boiled potatoes.

LIVER WITH DUBONNET AND ORANGE

Serves 2/245 calories per portion

225g/8oz calves' or lambs' liver, sliced 5mm/¼ inch thick, rinsed and drained
45ml/3 tablespoons red Dubonnet
5ml/1 level teaspoon finely grated orange rind
15ml/1 tablespoon fresh orange juice
30ml/2 tablespoons water
5ml/1 level teaspoon cornflour
Salt and pepper
5ml/1 level teaspoon chopped parsley

1. Place the liver in a single layer with the Dubonnet and orange rind. Cover with a lid or pierced cling film and microwave on HIGH for 1½ minutes.
2. Rearrange the pieces so that the outside pieces go to the centre. Cover again and microwave on HIGH for a further 1½ minutes. Remove the liver to a plate and cover with foil.
3. Mix orange juice and water with cornflour and stir into the juices in the dish. Microwave on HIGH for 1-1½ minutes until boiling and thickened, stirring briskly every 30 seconds.
4. Stir in the parsley and season to taste. Pour over the liver and serve.

Serving Suggestion:
A recipe to share, but a portion will keep in the refrigerator until the next day or freeze. Serve with broccoli at 35 calories for 150g/5oz weighed raw, and petit pois at 80 calories per 115g/4oz weighed frozen.

LAMB CASSEROLE

Serves 1/195 calories

25g/1oz onion, chopped
25g/1oz carrot, thinly
sliced
100ml/3½floz boiling
water
50g/2oz button
mushrooms, sliced
115g/4oz lamb leg steak or
boneless chop, trimmed of
all visible fat and cubed
½ lamb or beef stock cube
5ml/1 level teaspoon
tomato purée
1.25ml/¼ level teaspoon
dried rosemary
5ml/1 level teaspoon
cornflour
15ml/1 tablespoon cold
water
Salt and pepper

1. Place the onion and carrot in a small casserole dish with 30ml/2 tablespoons boiling water.
2. Cover with a lid or pierced cling film and microwave on HIGH for 2½ minutes.
3. Add the mushrooms and lamb. Dissolve the stock cube and tomato purée in the remaining boiling water and add to the dish with the rosemary.
4. Cover and cook on HIGH for 2 minutes. Stir, cover again, and cook on DEFROST for 15 minutes.
5. Mix the cornflour with the cold water and stir into the casserole. Cook on HIGH until boiling and thickened, stirring every 30 seconds. Leave to stand for 3 minutes.

Serving Suggestion:
A 150g/5oz potato boiled and mashed with 45ml/3 tablespoons skimmed milk will cost an extra 120 calories.

POSH PLAICE

Serves 1/215 calories

150g/5oz fillet of fresh
plaice, skinned
25g/1oz smoked salmon
⅛ fish or chicken stock
cube
60ml/4 tablespoons hot
water
15ml/1 level tablespoon
skimmed milk powder
Chopped parsley

1. Cut the plaice fillets into two strips. Cut smoked salmon into two strips and lay on each piece of plaice. Roll up tightly and place in a small dish.
2. Dissolve stock cube in 45ml/3 tablespoons hot water and pour over fish. Cover with a lid or pierced cling film and microwave on HIGH for 3 minutes. Leave to stand for 3 minutes.
3. Place fish on a serving plate. Cover and keep warm.
4. Blend skimmed milk powder with fish stock. Cover and cook on HIGH for 45 seconds, stirring twice.
5. Pour over fish and sprinkle with parsley.

Serving Suggestion:
A delicious treat which would go very well with broccoli and peas.

SPICY LAMB PILAFF

Serves 2/420 calories per portion

75g/3oz onion, chopped
5ml/1 teaspoon oil
15ml/1 tablespoon cold water
1 clove garlic, crushed
50g/2oz green or red pepper, deseeded and diced
7.5ml/1½ level teaspoons curry powder
4 cloves
2.5ml/½ level teaspoon chilli powder
1.25ml/¼ level teaspoon ground cinnamon
15ml/1 level tablespoon tomato purée
115g/4oz long-grain white rice
½ beef or lamb stock cube
275ml/½ pint boiling water
Pinch salt
75g/3oz frozen peas
150g/5oz roast lamb, trimmed of all visible fat and cut into small cubes

1. Place the onion, oil and cold water in a basin. Cover with a lid or pierced cling film and microwave on HIGH for 3 minutes.
2. Add the garlic and pepper. Cover again and cook for 1 minute.
3. Add the curry powder, cloves, chilli powder, cinnamon and tomato purée. Stir well, then add the rice.
4. Dissolve the stock cube in the boiling water and add to the dish with a pinch of salt. Cover and microwave on HIGH for 12 minutes.
5. Cover with foil and leave to stand for 5 minutes.
6. Stir in the peas and lamb. Cover and microwave on HIGH for 4 minutes.

Serving Suggestion:
If you are not sharing this pilaff you can save one portion in the refrigerator for reheating the next day. Serve on its own or with some lightly-boiled bean sprouts — 7 calories per 25g/1oz.

NEPTUNE'S PLAICE (See picture opposite page 65)

Serves 1/305 calories

150g/5oz fillet of plaice
10ml/2 level teaspoons lemon juice
50g/1.76oz potted shrimps
Lemon wedges

1. Place fish in a dish with lemon juice and top with potted shrimps. Cover with a lid or pierced cling film and microwave on HIGH for 3 minutes.
2. Leave to stand for 3 minutes.
3. Serve with wedges of lemon.

Serving Suggestion:
115g/4oz courgettes, sliced and boiled would add just 15 calories. Or slice the courgettes and sprinkle with about 5ml/1 teaspoon Burgess Mushroom Ketchup, cover and cook on HIGH in the microwave for 3 minutes.

PORK IN BLACKBERRY AND PORT SAUCE

Serves 4/225 calories per portion

**575g/1¼lb pork tenderloin or fillet, trimmed of fat
150ml/¼ pint boiling water
½ chicken stock cube
225g/8oz blackberries, fresh or frozen
90ml/6 tablespoons water
15ml/1 level tablespoon redcurrant jelly
30ml/2 tablespoons port
10ml/2 level teaspoons arrowroot**

1. Cut the pork into four even-sized pieces. Place in a dish.
2. Dissolve the stock cube in boiling water and pour over pork. Cover with a lid or pierced cling film and microwave on HIGH for 4 minutes.
3. Rearrange the pieces, then cook for a further 4 minutes. Cover dish with foil and leave to stand while you make the sauce.
4. Place frozen blackberries in a dish and microwave on DEFROST for 5 minutes, stirring halfway through.
5. Add 60ml/4 tablespoons water to defrosted or fresh blackberries and cover with a lid or pierced cling film. Microwave on HIGH for 3 minutes or until tender.
6. Purée blackberries in a blender or food processor, then rub through a sieve to remove the pips.
7. Stir in the redcurrant jelly and port.
8. Mix 30ml/2 tablespoons water with the arrowroot and add to the purée. Cook on HIGH until boiling, stirring every 30 seconds.
9. Drain off any liquid from the meat and discard. Pour the blackberry sauce over the pork. Cover and microwave on HIGH for 5 minutes.

Serving Suggestion:
An extra special dish that you could serve on special occasions. Delicious with boiled broccoli and cauliflower.

PORK CASSEROLE WITH SAGE DUMPLINGS

Serves 1/395 calories

40g/1½oz carrot, thinly sliced
25g/1oz onion, chopped
90ml/6 tablespoons boiling water
115g/4oz pork fillet or tenderloin, trimmed of fat and cubed
25g/1oz button mushrooms, quartered
¼ chicken stock cube
5ml/1 level teaspoon tomato purée
5ml/1 level teaspoon cornflour
Salt and pepper
25g/1oz self-raising flour
15g/½oz shredded suet
1.25ml/¼ level teaspoon dried sage

1. Place the carrot and onion in a small casserole dish with 30ml/2 tablespoons boiling water. Cover with a lid or pierced cling film and microwave on HIGH for 2½ minutes.
2. Add the pork and mushrooms. Dissolve the stock cube and tomato purée in 60ml/4 tablespoons boiling water and add to the dish. Cover and microwave on HIGH for 5 minutes, stirring after 2½ minutes.
3. Mix the cornflour with 15ml/1 tablespoon cold water until smooth, then stir into the casserole. Microwave on HIGH until boiling and thickened, stirring every 30 seconds. Season lightly with salt and pepper.
4. Mix the flour, suet and sage together and season. Add enough cold water to make a firm dough. Shape into two dumplings and place in the casserole. Cover and microwave on HIGH for 4 minutes.

Serving Suggestion:
A substantial casserole which could be served on its own or add a few cooked greens.

MEDITERRANEAN PLAICE

Serves 1/165 calories

¼ red or green pepper, deseeded and diced
1 medium courgette, thinly sliced
1 spring onion, trimmed and thinly sliced
75ml/3floz tomato juice
Pinch dried basil or mixed herbs
Salt and pepper
150g/5oz plaice fillets, thawed if frozen

1. Place all the vegetables in a dish large enough to hold the plaice in a single layer. Add tomato juice and basil. Season with salt and pepper. Cover dish with a lid or pierced cling film and microwave on HIGH for 5 minutes.
2. Lay the plaice on top of the vegetables in a single layer. Cover and microwave on HIGH for a further 2 minutes or until fish flakes easily.

Serving Suggestion:
Ideal with a helping of boiled potatoes. You could afford to add 225g/8oz potatoes and still have a meal that costs under 400 calories.

PORK IN YOGURT AND MUSTARD SAUCE

Serves 1/245 calories

115g/4oz lean pork fillet
or tenderloin, trimmed of
all visible fat and cut into
small strips
5ml/1 level teaspoon
cornflour
5ml/1 level teaspoon
butter
2.5ml/½ teaspoon oil
50g/2oz button
mushrooms, sliced
2 spring onions, trimmed
and sliced
30ml/2 level tablespoons
natural low-fat yogurt
1.25ml/¼ level teaspoon
French mustard
Salt and pepper

1. Toss pork in the cornflour until all pieces are coated.
2. Place the butter and oil in a small casserole dish. Cover with a lid or pierced cling film and microwave on HIGH until melted — about 1 minute.
3. Add the meat and turn all the pieces in the butter. Arrange in a single layer. Cover and microwave on HIGH for 1½ minutes.
4. Rearrange the pieces, cover again and microwave on HIGH for a further 1½ minutes.
5. Stir in the mushrooms and spring onions. Cover and microwave on HIGH for 1½ minutes. Leave to stand for 1½ minutes.
6. Mix together the yogurt and mustard and stir into the pork. Season. Microwave on high for 30 seconds.

Serving Suggestion:
Try with tagliatelle or egg noodles. If you buy the dried sort, count 105 calories per 25g/1oz before cooking. Fresh tagliatelle or noodles cost 80 calories per 25g/1oz but won't absorb as much water in cooking so you'll need more. Allow yourself 25g/1oz pasta weighed dry or 50g/2oz fresh pasta.

PLAICE WITH CRUMB TOPPING

Serves 1/280 calories

175g/6oz plaice fillets,
fresh or defrosted
1 tomato, sliced
25g/1oz fat-reduced hard
cheese, grated
15g/½oz fresh wholemeal
breadcrumbs
5ml/1 level teaspoon
chopped parsley
Salt and pepper

1. Arrange the plaice fillets in a fairly shallow dish, tucking any thin parts underneath. Cover with a lid or pierced cling film and microwave on HIGH for 1½ minutes.
2. Arrange tomato on top to cover the fish. Cover and microwave on HIGH for 1 minute.
3. Pour off any cooking juices and discard. Leave to stand for 1½ minutes.
4. Mix cheese with the breadcrumbs and parsley. Season, then sprinkle over the fish. Microwave on HIGH for 1½ minutes.
5. Serve immediately or brown under the grill.

Serving Suggestion:
Add 115g/4oz sweetcorn, frozen or canned, for an extra 100 calories.

INDIVIDUAL MEAT LOAF

Serves 1/330 calories

**150g/5oz very lean ground or minced beef
15g/½oz wholemeal breadcrumbs
5ml/1 teaspoon milk
15ml/1 level tablespoon tomato ketchup
2.5ml/½ level teaspoon Worcestershire sauce
25g/1oz mushrooms, very finely chopped
Salt and pepper**

1. Mix all the ingredients thoroughly together.
2. Place in a small basin or dish. Microwave on HIGH for 3½ minutes.
3. Leave to stand for 2 minutes.
4. Turn out and discard any fat that runs out. Serve hot or cold.

Serving Suggestion:
If you are serving hot add some microwaved or boiled vegetables. If you are serving cold add a salad.

BROCCOLI AND COD AU GRATIN

Serves 1/380 calories

**115g/4oz broccoli, fresh or frozen
15ml/1 tablespoon water
175g/6oz cod fillet, fresh or defrosted
Squeeze of lemon juice
150ml/¼ pint skimmed milk
15ml/1 level tablespoon cornflour
25g/1oz mature Cheddar cheese, grated
Salt and pepper
Little mustard
30ml/2 level tablespoons fresh wholemeal breadcrumbs**

1. Place the broccoli in a dish with the water. Cover with a lid or pierced cling film and microwave on HIGH for 4 minutes. Drain off any excess liquid. Cover the broccoli with foil and set aside.
2. Place the cod in a dish and squeeze on a little lemon juice. Cover with a lid or pierced cling film and microwave on HIGH for 1½ minutes or until fish flakes easily.
3. Place fish on the broccoli and cover with foil while you make the sauce.
4. Blend the cornflour with a little milk until smooth, then stir in the remaining milk. Microwave on HIGH until boiling and thickened, stirring well every 30 seconds. Stir in the cheese and season to taste.
5. Pour sauce over the fish. Sprinkle the crumbs on top and microwave on HIGH for 1 minute.
6. Place under the grill to brown the breadcrumbs.

Serving Suggestion:
A complete meal in itself, but you could add a crisp green side salad if you wish.

SAVOURY MINCE WITH DUMPLINGS

Serves 4/420 calories per portion

50g/2oz celery, thinly sliced
115g/4oz onion, chopped
75g/3oz carrot, thinly sliced
30ml/2 tablespoons cold water
450g/1lb very lean ground or minced beef
30ml/2 level tablespoons plain flour
1 beef stock cube
15ml/1 level tablespoon tomato purée
200ml/7floz boiling water
5ml/1 level teaspoon mixed dried herbs
Salt and pepper
75g/3oz self-raising flour
40g/1½oz shredded suet

1. Place the celery, onion and carrot in a casserole dish with the 30ml/2 tablespoons cold water. Cover with a lid or pierced cling film and microwave on HIGH for 3 minutes.
2. Stir, cover again and cook on HIGH for a further 2 minutes.
3. Stir in the beef. Cover and cook on HIGH for 5 minutes.
4. Stir in the flour until well mixed, breaking up any large clumps of meat.
5. Dissolve the stock cube and tomato purée in the boiling water. Add to the casserole with the herbs. Cover and cook on HIGH for 5 minutes. Stir, then cover and cook on HIGH for a further 5 minutes.
6. Stir, then leave to stand for 5 minutes. Season to taste.
7. Sieve the self-raising flour with a pinch of salt. Stir in the suet, then add enough water to make a firm dough. Shape into four dumplings, using floured hands, and place on top of the meat.
8. Cover and cook on HIGH for 5 minutes.

Serving Suggestion:
Add any greens. A 175g/6oz helping of boiled and chopped cabbage will add just 25 calories.

SPICY MEATBALLS

Serves 1/315 calories

150g/5oz very lean ground or minced beef
5ml/1 level teaspoon garam masala
15ml/1 level tablespoon mango chutney
Salt and pepper
25g/1oz onion, finely chopped
150ml/¼ pint water
5ml/1 level teaspoon curry powder
2.5ml/½ level teaspoon turmeric
5ml/1 level teaspoon grated fresh root ginger
¼ beef stock cube
5ml/1 level teaspoon cornflour

1. Mix the beef with the garam masala and mango chutney. Season and shape into four balls. Arrange on a shallow dish and cover with a lid or pierced cling film. Microwave on HIGH for 3¼ minutes.
2. Drain off any fat that cooks out. Cover meatballs with foil while you make the sauce.
3. Place the onion in a dish with 30ml/2 tablespoons water. Cover and cook on HIGH for 2 minutes.
4. Stir in the curry powder, turmeric and ginger and cook on HIGH for 1 minute.
5. Add 75ml/5 tablespoons water and the crumbled stock cube. Cook on HIGH for 2 minutes.
6. Blend the cornflour with the remaining water and stir into the sauce. Cook on HIGH for 1½ minutes, stirring briskly every 20 seconds.
7. Add the meatballs. Cover and cook on HIGH for 1 minute.

Serving Suggestion:
Boil 25g/1oz brown rice and serve with meatballs. This will bring your meal's total up to 415 calories.

CORNED BEEF AND POTATO HASH

Serves 1/345 calories

115g/4oz potato, peeled weight
15ml/1 tablespoon water
75g/3oz corned beef
1 pickled onion
30ml/2 level tablespoons piccalilli
15g/½oz reduced-fat hard cheese, grated

1. Slice the potato and arrange, overlapping in the base of a small dish. Add the water. Cover with a lid or pierced cling film and microwave on HIGH for 4 minutes. Leave to stand for 2 minutes, then drain off any excess water.
2. Chop the corned beef and pickled onion. Mix with the piccalilli and spread over the potato.
3. Sprinkle cheese on top. Microwave on HIGH for 2 minutes.

Serving Suggestion:
There is no need to add anything to this dish, but if you wish you can accompany it with shredded iceberg lettuce or boiled green beans.

BEEF IN OYSTER SAUCE (See picture opposite page 64)

Serves 2/275 calories per portion

225g/8oz lean beef, flash or quick fry
50g/2oz red pepper
50g/2oz green pepper
115g/4oz carrots
75g/3oz baby sweetcorn
75g/3oz peas or mangetout
30ml/2 tablespoons Sharwood's oyster sauce
15ml/1 tablespoon soy sauce
30ml/2 tablespoons dry sherry
60ml/4 tablespoons water
10ml/2 level teaspoons cornflour
Salt and pepper
115g/4oz mushrooms, thinly sliced
115g/4oz courgettes, thinly sliced
4 spring onions, trimmed and finely chopped

1. Cut the beef into bite-sized cubes and deseeded pepper and carrots into short strips. Trim baby sweetcorn and mangetout.
2. Mix together the oyster sauce, soy sauce, sherry, water and cornflour. Season to taste.
3. Place the meat in microwave dish and cook for 4 minutes on HIGH, stirring after 2 minutes.
4. Add the sauces and cook for 3 minutes on HIGH, stirring once.
5. Stir in all the vegetables and cook for further 5 minutes on HIGH, stirring once.

Serving Suggestion:
A complete meal on its own.

POACHED SALMON

Serves 1/210 calories

1 salmon steak, about 175g/6oz
15ml/1 tablespoon water
2.5ml/½ level teaspoon low-fat spread

1. Place the salmon steak in a dish with the thin part towards the centre.
2. Pour over the water and dot with spread.
3. Cover with a lid or pierced cling film and microwave on HIGH for 2 minutes.

Serving Suggestion:
Lovely with boiled tiny new potatoes and a crisp green salad. For an easy sauce costing just 50 calories extra, try this: Mix together 30ml/2 level tablespoons fromage frais, 15ml/1 level tablespoon strained Greek-style yogurt, a pinch of dried dill weed and season with salt and pepper to taste.

MEATBALLS IN TOMATO SAUCE

Serves 1/410 calories

150g/5oz very lean ground
or minced beef
15g/½oz fresh
breadcrumbs
15ml/1 level tablespoon
tomato ketchup
1.25ml/¼ level teaspoon
mixed dried herbs or
2.5ml/½ level teaspoon
fresh herbs
15ml/1 level tablespoon
grated Parmesan cheese
Salt and pepper
25g/1oz onion, finely
chopped
25g/1oz red or green
pepper, deseeded and
diced
150ml/¼ pint tomato juice
Pinch dried oregano
¼ beef stock cube
5ml/1 level teaspoon
cornflour

1. Mix the beef with the breadcrumbs, tomato ketchup, herbs, Parmesan cheese and salt and pepper. It is easiest to do this with your hand. Shape mixture into four balls.
2. Arrange meatballs around the edge of a shallow dish. Microwave on HIGH for 2 minutes.
3. Turn the meatballs over and rearrange them. Microwave on HIGH for a further 1¼ minutes. Drain off any fat that runs out. Cover the meatballs with foil while you make the sauce.
4. Place the onion in a small dish with 30ml/2 tablespoons tomato juice. Cover and cook on HIGH for 2 minutes.
5. Add the pepper to the onion with the oregano. Cover and cook on HIGH for 1 minute.
6. Stir in the crumbled stock cube and 75ml/5 tablespoons tomato juice. Cover and microwave on HIGH for 1 minute.
7. Blend the cornflour with remaining tomato juice, then stir into the sauce. Cook on HIGH until boiled and thickened, stirring well every 20 seconds. Season.
8. Pour sauce over the meatballs. Cover loosely and cook on HIGH for 1 minute.

Serving Suggestion:
Cauliflower florets can fill your plate at a minimum calorie cost. A 175g/6oz helping weighed raw, then boiled will cost 25 calories. That brings your meal total up to 435 calories.

LIVER IN ONION SAUCE

Serves 1/270 calories

50g/2oz onion, finely chopped
105ml/7 tablespoons cold water
¼ lamb or beef stock cube
115g/4oz lamb's liver, sliced 5mm/¼ inch thick and trimmed of tubes
30ml/2 level tablespoons skimmed milk powder
5ml/1 level teaspoon cornflour

1. Place the onion in a dish large enough to contain the liver in one layer. Add 30ml/2 tablespoons water. Cover with a lid or pierced cling film and microwave on HIGH for 4 minutes. Stir after 2 minutes.
2. Stir in the crumbled stock cube.
3. Wash liver in cold water and pat dry with kitchen paper. Add to the onion, arranging the slices in a single layer. Cover and cook on HIGH for 1 minute.
4. Rearrange the pieces of liver, cover again and cook on HIGH for a further minute.
5. Remove the liver to a warm place and cover with foil.
6. Blend the skimmed milk powder with cornflour and remaining 75ml/5 tablespoons cold water. Stir into the onion and cook on HIGH for 2 minutes, stirring briskly every 30 seconds.
7. Pour the onion sauce over the liver and serve.

Serving Suggestion:
Add boiled potatoes and carrots. Or serve with a frozen cauliflower, peas and carrot mixture about 10 calories per 28g/1oz.

KIDNEYS PROVENÇALE (See picture opposite page 65)

Serves 1/170 calories

½ medium onion, sliced
1 small carrot, sliced
225g/8oz can chopped tomatoes
10ml/2 level teaspoons tomato purée
115g/4oz lambs' kidneys, cored and halved
25g/1oz mushrooms, sliced
¼ green pepper, deseeded and sliced
½ clove garlic, crushed
Pinch mixed herbs
5ml/1 level teaspoon cornflour

1. Place the onion and carrot in a dish with contents of the can of tomatoes and tomato purée.
2. Cover and microwave on HIGH for 4 minutes.
3. Place the kidneys, mushrooms, green pepper, garlic and herbs in the dish.
4. Cover with a lid or pierced cling film and microwave on HIGH for 2 minutes.
5. Blend cornflour with a little cold water and stir into the casserole. Cover and cook on HIGH for 1½ minutes, stirring twice.
6. Cover and leave to stand for 3 minutes.

Serving Suggestion:
Good with boiled rice (35 calories for 25g/1oz weighed cooked). Boiled rice can be cooked and frozen in portions ready for reheating in the microwave.

LIVER AND SAUSAGE CASSEROLE WITH BEANS

Serves 4/355 calories per portion

40g/1½ oz streaky bacon
2 pork sausages, pricked
75g/3oz carrots, thinly sliced
75g/3oz onion, chopped
60ml/4 tablespoons cold water
227g/8oz can tomatoes, roughly chopped
350g/12oz lambs' liver or pigs' liver, trimmed of tubes
2.5ml/½ level teaspoon mixed dried herbs
150ml/¼ pint boiling water
1 beef stock cube
5ml/1 teaspoon Worcestershire sauce
30ml/2 level tablespoons cornflour
454g/1lb can baked beans in tomato sauce
Salt and pepper

1. Place the bacon between two double pieces of kitchen paper. Microwave on HIGH for 2 minutes. Cut into small pieces.
2. Place the sausages on a plate and cover with a double thickness of kitchen paper. Microwave on HIGH for 3 minutes. Drain off and discard any fat that runs out.
3. Place the carrot and onion in a casserole dish with 30ml/2 tablespoons of water. Cover with a lid or pierced cling film and microwave on HIGH for 5 minutes.
4. Add the tomatoes and their juice.
5. Slice the liver fairly thinly and arrange in the dish in an even layer. Sprinkle on the herbs.
6. Dissolve the stock cube in the boiling water with the Worcestershire sauce.
7. Mix the cornflour with the remaining 30ml/2 tablespoons cold water, then stir into the stock. Microwave on HIGH until boiling, stirring briskly every 30 seconds. Pour over the meat and vegetables. Microwave on HIGH for 8 minutes.
8. Slice the sausages thickly. Stir into the casserole with the bacon and baked beans. Microwave on HIGH for 4 minutes.

Serving Suggestion:
A tasty family meal which is quite economical too. Serve with Brussels sprouts counting 30 calories for a 175g/6oz boiled serving.

KIDNEYS AND BUTTER BEAN CURRY

Serves 1/320 calories

25g/1oz onion, chopped
5ml/1 teaspoon oil
½-1 small clove garlic,
crushed
2.5ml/½ level teaspoon
grated fresh root ginger
5ml/1 level teaspoon curry
powder
115g/4oz lambs' kidneys,
halved, cored
30ml/2 level tablespoons
tomato chutney
75ml/3floz hot water
115g/4oz canned butter
beans, drained
5ml/1 level teaspoon
cornflour
60ml/4 tablespoons cold
water
Salt and pepper

1. Place the onion in a small dish with the oil. Stir to mix. Cover with a lid or pierced cling film and cook on HIGH for 1½ minutes.
2. Add garlic to onion with ginger and curry powder. Stir to mix. Cover and cook on HIGH for 1 minute.
3. Cut each kidney half into 4 pieces. Add to dish with tomato chutney and water. Cover and cook on HIGH for 3 minutes.
4. Stir in the butter beans.
5. Blend cornflour with cold water and stir into the dish. Cook on HIGH for 1½ minutes, stirring every 30 seconds.

Serving Suggestion:
Finely shredded raw white cabbage will complement a curry and cost few calories — 6 per 28g/1oz.

DEVILLED LIVER

Serves 1/265 calories

115g/4oz lamb's liver,
sliced 5mm/¼ inch thick
and trimmed of tubes
1 clove garlic, crushed
10ml/2 level teaspoons
low-fat spread
5ml/1 teaspoon
Worcestershire sauce
20ml/4 level teaspoons
tomato ketchup
5ml/1 level teaspoon
horseradish sauce
2.5ml/½ level teaspoon
dry mustard powder

1. Wash the liver in cold water and pat dry with kitchen paper. Place in a single layer in a fairly shallow dish.
2. Mix the garlic with the low-fat spread, Worcestershire sauce, tomato ketchup, horseradish sauce and dry mustard powder. Spread half of this paste over the liver. Cover with a lid or pierced cling film (ensuring that it does not touch the liver), and microwave on HIGH for 1 minute.
3. Turn the liver slices over. Spread with remaining paste. Cover and microwave on HIGH for a further 30 seconds. Leave to stand covered, for 1 minute.
4. Stir the juices in the dish and spoon over the liver.

Serving Suggestion:
Serve with mushrooms poached in water or stock — 115g/4oz costs 15 calories plus a portion of ratatouille (see page 66).

KIDNEYS AND SHERRY CASSEROLE

Serves 1/150 calories

25g/1oz onion, chopped
15ml/1 tablespoon cold
water
115g/4oz lambs' kidneys,
halved, cored and skinned
¼ beef stock cube
75ml/3floz boiling water
50g/2oz mushrooms,
quartered if large
15ml/1 tablespoon sherry
5ml/1 level teaspoon
cornflour
Salt and pepper

1. Place the onion in a small casserole dish with the cold water. Cover with a lid or pierced cling film. Microwave on HIGH for 2 minutes.
2. Place kidneys on onion in a single layer.
3. Dissolve stock cube in boiling water and pour over kidneys. Cover dish again and microwave on HIGH for 2 minutes.
4. Add mushrooms to dish, cover again and cook on HIGH for 1 minute.
5. Blend cornflour with sherry and stir into casserole. Microwave on HIGH for 1½ minutes, stirring briskly every 30 seconds. Season to taste with salt and pepper.

Serving Suggestion:
Add a 200g/7oz potato baked in its jacket and your meal's total will still be only 300 calories. Bake your potato in the microwave first, then wrap in foil and keep warm in the oven until the casserole is cooked.

KIDNEYS AND BACON IN TOMATO SAUCE

Serves 1/200 calories

25g/1oz streaky bacon
25g/1oz onion, finely
chopped
45ml/3 tablespoons water
115g/4oz lambs' kidneys,
halved, cored and sliced
¼ beef or lamb stock cube
1.25ml/¼ level teaspoon
dried oregano or
2.5ml/½ level teaspoon
chopped fresh oregano
75ml/3floz tomato juice
25g/1oz green or red
pepper, deseeded and
sliced
5ml/1 level teaspoon
cornflour

1. Place the bacon between two double layers of kitchen paper and microwave on HIGH for 1¼-1½ minutes until well cooked. Cut into small pieces.
2. Place the onion in a small casserole dish with 30ml/2 tablespoons water. Cover with a lid or pierced cling film and microwave on HIGH for 2 minutes.
3. Add the kidneys, crumbled stock cube, oregano and tomato juice. Mix well. Cover and microwave on HIGH for 2 minutes.
4. Stir pepper into dish. Cover and microwave on HIGH for 1½ minutes.
5. Add the bacon.
6. Mix the cornflour with 15ml/1 tablespoon water and stir into the dish. Microwave on HIGH until boiling, stirring briskly every 30 seconds.

Serving Suggestion:
A 115g/4oz helping boiled broad beans adds 120 calories and complements this casserole.

KEDGEREE

Serves 2/430 calories per portion

175g/6oz smoked
haddock, fresh or
defrosted
30ml/2 tablespoons water
10ml/2 level teaspoons
butter
5ml/1 level teaspoon curry
powder
115g/4oz long-grain white
rice
275ml/½ pint boiling
water
115g/4oz frozen peas
Black pepper
2 eggs, size 3, hard-boiled

1. Place the smoked haddock in a shallow dish and tuck any thin parts underneath. Add the water, cover with a lid or pierced cling film and microwave on HIGH for 1½ minutes.
2. Place the butter in another dish and microwave on HIGH for 30 to 40 seconds until melted.
3. Stir in the curry powder and microwave on HIGH for 30 seconds.
4. Add the rice, boiling water and liquid from the fish. Cover and microwave on HIGH for 10 minutes.
5. Stir in the peas and season with pepper. Microwave on HIGH for 3 minutes.
6. Skin and flake the smoked haddock and stir into the rice. Microwave on HIGH for 1 minute.
7. Cover dish with foil, shiny side down, and leave to stand for 4 minutes.
8. Shell and roughly chop the eggs. Stir into the kedgeree and serve.

Serving Suggestion:
Makes a substantial meal on its own. If you are not sharing you can save one portion in the refrigerator until the next day.

SEAFOOD PILAFF

Serves 2/435 calories per portion

**25g/1oz onion, chopped
10ml/2 level teaspoons
butter
15ml/1 tablespoon cold
water
2.5ml/½ level teaspoon
dried mixed herbs
50g/2oz button
mushrooms, sliced
50g/2oz red pepper,
deseeded and diced
115g/4oz long-grain white
rice
½ chicken stock cube
275ml/½ pint boiling
water
175g/6oz cod or haddock
fillet, fresh or defrosted,
cubed
115g/4oz frozen peas
75g/3oz prawns, thawed if
frozen
75g/3oz mussels, canned
in natural juice or brine,
drained
Salt and pepper**

1. Place the onion, butter and cold water in a bowl. Cover with a lid or pierced cling film and microwave on HIGH for 2 minutes. Add the herbs, mushrooms, pepper and rice.
2. Dissolve the stock cube in the boiling water and add to the dish. Cover and microwave on HIGH for 8 minutes.
3. Add the cod or haddock fillet and peas. Cover and microwave on HIGH for 5 minutes.
4. Cover with foil and leave to stand for 5 minutes. Drain off any any excess liquid.
5. Stir in the mussels and prawns. Cover and microwave on HIGH for 2 minutes.

Serving Suggestion:
A tasty pilaff to which you don't need to add anything. The second portion could be eaten cold the next day if you wish.

HALIBUT IN PRAWN SAUCE

Serves 4/320 calories

575ml/1 pint skimmed milk
1 bay leaf
1 small carrot
Slice of onion
8 peppercorns
Sprig of parsley
2 inch piece of celery
575g/1¼lb halibut fillet, skinned and cut into 4 even-sized pieces
60ml/4 level tablespoons cornflour
50g/2oz Gruyére cheese, grated
115g/4oz prawns, thawed if frozen and drained
Salt
Mild paprika

1. Place 525ml/18floz milk in a large jug. Add the bay leaf, carrot, onion, peppercorns, parsley and celery. Cover with a lid or pierced cling film and microwave on HIGH until almost boiling — about 3 minutes. Leave to stand for 10 minutes.
2. Place halibut in a shallow dish in a single layer with the thinner parts in the centre. Cover and microwave on HIGH for 5½ minutes — or until the fish flakes easily. Cover with foil and leave to stand while you make the sauce.
3. Mix the cornflour with the remaining milk until smooth. Strain the infused milk onto the cornflour mixture, stirring, and then return to the jug. Microwave on HIGH until boiling and thickened — about 5 minutes, stirring briskly every 30 seconds.
4. Stir in the cheese and prawns and add salt to taste. Drain any liquid from the fish and discard. Pour sauce over the fish and sprinkle with mild paprika.

Serving Suggestion:
A deliciously special recipe that deserves some extra-special vegetables. Baby new potatoes, mange tout, broccoli would all go well.

PIQUANT FISH CUSTARD

Serves 1/315 calories

160g/5½oz cod or haddock fillet
5ml/1 level teaspoon capers, chopped
5ml/1 level teaspoon chopped gherkins
150ml/¼ pint natural low-fat yogurt
1 egg, size 3
15ml/1 level tablespoon cornflour
2.5ml/½ level teaspoon grated lemon rind
Salt and pepper

1. Place the fish in a small dish and cover with a lid or pierced cling film. Microwave on HIGH for 1½ minutes.
2. Discard any liquid and divide the fish into large flakes.
3. Beat all the remaining ingredients together until evenly mixed. Pour over the fish.
4. Place the dish in a larger dish containing enough hot water to come level with the custard. Microwave on HIGH for 4½ minutes.
5. Cook on DEFROST for 5 minutes. Then leave to stand for 5 minutes.

Serving Suggestion:
Serve with a green salad and sliced tomatoes.

CHILLI CON CARNE

Serves 4/320 calories per portion

450g/1lb very lean minced or ground beef
115g/4oz onion, chopped
115g/4oz red pepper, deseeded and diced
396g/14oz can chopped tomatoes
10ml/2 level teaspoons chilli powder, mild or hot
2.5ml/½ level teaspoon ground cumin
2.5ml/½ level teaspoon ground coriander
10ml/2 level teaspoons brown sugar
½ beef stock cube
425g/15oz can red kidney beans, drained
Salt and pepper

1. Place the meat in a bowl and break up with a fork. Cover with a lid or pierced cling film and microwave on HIGH for 2 minutes.
2. Stir in the onion. Cover and microwave on HIGH for 2 minutes.
3. Add the red pepper, tomatoes, chilli powder, cumin, coriander, brown sugar and crumbled stock cube. Cover and microwave on HIGH for 3 minutes.
4. Stir well, then cover again and microwave on HIGH for a further 3 minutes.
5. Stir again. Cover and microwave on HIGH for 4 minutes.
6. Add the drained beans. Cover and microwave on HIGH for 4 minutes.
7. Taste and season with salt and pepper if necessary. Leave to stand for 5 minutes.

Serving Suggestion:
Chilli con Carne is hot, filling and a very satisfying dieting dish which the whole family can share. You could afford to add a 50g/2oz helping of boiled rice and still keep total calories under 400.

PORK FILLET WITH CUMBRIAN SAUCE
(See picture opposite page 65)

Serves 1/280 calories

115g/4oz pork fillet or tenderloin, fat removed
25ml/5 level teaspoons redcurrant jelly
Rind ½ orange
15ml/1 tablespoon orange juice
30ml/2 tablespoons water
15ml/1 tablespoon port
5ml/1 level teaspoon cornflour

1. Place pork fillet in a shallow dish. Cover with a lid or pierced cling and microwave on HIGH for 4 minutes.
2. Leave to stand.
3. Place redcurrant jelly and orange rind in a jug, cover and microwave on HIGH for 30 seconds.
4. Stir in orange juice and water. Blend port and cornflour together and stir into other ingredients. Cover and microwave on HIGH for 1 minute, stirring twice during cooking.
5. Slice pork thinly, cover with the sauce and serve.

Serving Suggestion:
Add 75g/3oz frozen peas and 75g/3oz cauliflower, both boiled or steamed, for a meal costing a total of 340 calories.

TROUT IN ORANGE SAUCE

Serves 1/205 calories

1 trout, 200g/7oz, thawed if frozen
15ml/1 tablespoon lemon juice
Pepper
50ml/2floz orange juice
3.75ml/¾ level teaspoon cornflour

1. Wash the trout in cold water and pat dry with kitchen paper.
2. Place on a piece of cling film and sprinkle on 5ml/1 teaspoon lemon juice and a little pepper. Wrap up to make a loose parcel and pierce once. Place on a plate and microwave on HIGH for 2½ minutes.
3. Turn the fish over and cook on HIGH for a further 2½ minutes.
4. Unwrap fish and place on a warm plate. Cover with foil and leave to stand while you make the sauce.
5. Place orange juice in a jug and microwave on HIGH for 1½ minutes.
6. Blend cornflour with the remaining lemon juice, then stir into the orange juice. Microwave on HIGH for 1 minute, stirring briskly every 20 seconds, or until boiling and thickened.
7. Pour sauce over trout and serve.

Serving Suggestion:
Good with green beans and boiled swedes if they are in season. Count 5 calories per boiled 28g/1oz of each.

VEGETABLE VARIATIONS

You don't have to be a vegetarian to enjoy the meals you'll find in this chapter. And most of the meals are complete so you don't have to bother with cooking separate accompaniments. Also included in this section are some creative vegetable mixes which will really brighten up a meal if you serve them with sliced leftover cooked meats, poultry or with plain grilled or microwaved fish steaks.

VEGETABLE AND CHEESE PIE

Serves 1/405 calories

75g/3oz carrots, thinly sliced
45ml/3 tablespoons water
75g/3oz broad beans, weighed without pods
75g/3oz courgettes, thinly sliced
15ml/1 level tablespoon cornflour
150ml/¼ pint skimmed milk
50g/2oz reduced-fat Cheddar cheese, grated
15g/½oz fresh wholemeal breadcrumbs
Salt, pepper and mustard

1. Place the carrots in a serving dish with 15ml/1 tablespoon water. Cover with a lid or pierced cling film and microwave on HIGH for 2 minutes.
2. Add the broad beans. Stir, then cover and microwave on HIGH for a further 2 minutes.
3. Stir in the courgettes. Cover and microwave on HIGH for 3 minutes. Stir, cover again and cook on HIGH for 2 minutes.
4. Cover with foil and leave to stand while you make the sauce.
5. Blend the cornflour with a little skimmed milk, then stir in the remaining milk.
6. Microwave on HIGH until boiling and thickened, about 2 minutes, stirring briskly every 30 seconds.
7. Add most of the cheese to the sauce. Season with pepper and a little mustard. Taste and add salt if necessary.
8. Drain the water from the vegetables, then stir them into the sauce.
9. Sprinkle the remaining cheese and crumbs on top and grill until brown.

Serving Suggestion:
Makes a substantial meal on its own.

POTATO SALAD

Serves 1/185 calories

175g/6oz new potatoes
30ml/2 tablespoons water
2 radishes, sliced
1 stick celery, sliced
1 spring onion, leaves discarded, sliced
30ml/2 level tablespoons low-fat natural yogurt
15ml/1 level tablespoon low calorie salad dressing
Salt and pepper

1. Scrub the potatoes and place in a dish with the water. Cover with a lid or pierced cling film and microwave on HIGH for 5 minutes rearranging after 2½ minutes.
2. Drain and leave to cool.
3. Mix the radishes, celery and spring onion with the potatoes.
4. Mix together the yogurt and low calorie salad dressing. Season to taste with salt and pepper, then stir into the salad.

Serving Suggestion:
Makes a filling light meal on its own, or non-vegetarians could serve the salad with cold sliced chicken or lean ham to make it into a main meal.

BEETROOT IN PINK CHEESE SAUCE

Serves 1/365 calories

150g/5oz raw beetroot
30ml/2 tablespoons water
150ml/¼ pint skimmed milk
15ml/1 level tablespoon cornflour
50g/2oz Red Windsor or red-veined Cheddar cheese, grated
Salt and pepper
15ml/1 level tablespoon fresh wholemeal breadcrumbs

1. Wash and prick the beetroot but do not peel it. Wrap it loosely in cling film to make a parcel. Pierce the cling film. Microwave on HIGH for 2½ minutes.
2. Turn beetroot over and microwave on HIGH for a further 2½ minutes or until tender. Leave to stand for 2 minutes.
3. Mix milk with the cornflour and microwave on HIGH until boiling and thickened — about 2½ minutes, stirring every 30 seconds.
4. Stir the cheese into the sauce. Season to taste with salt and pepper.
5. Drain and peel beetroot. Slice and place in a dish. Pour the sauce on top. Sprinkle with the breadcrumbs. Grill until they are crisp.

Serving Suggestion:
Eat with a couple of crispbreads if you wish.

BEAN RISOTTO

Serves 1/340 calories

50g/2oz long-grain white rice
1.25ml/¼ level teaspoon ground cumin
1.25ml/¼ level teaspoon chilli powder, hot or mild
½ chicken stock cube
10ml/2 level teaspoons tomato purée
225ml/8floz boiling water
25g/1oz onion, chopped
50g/2oz green or red pepper, diced
115g/4oz drained canned red kidney beans

1. Mix the rice with the cumin and chilli powder in a deep bowl.
2. Dissolve the stock cube and tomato purée in the boiling water and add to the rice. Cover with a lid or pierced cling film and microwave on HIGH for 6 minutes.
3. Place the onion and pepper in a small bowl, cover and microwave on HIGH for 2 minutes. Add to the rice.
4. Stir the beans into the rice. Cover and microwave on HIGH for a further 2½ minutes.
5. Leave to stand, covered, until all the stock is absorbed.

Serving Suggestion:
A filling main meal which doesn't need any extras.

NOODLES WITH MUSHROOM SAUCE

Serves 1/350 calories

75g/3oz fresh noodles
225ml/8floz boiling water
Salt and pepper
75g/3oz button
mushrooms, sliced
1 bay leaf
Bouquet garni
45ml/3 level tablespoons
skimmed milk powder
15ml/1 level tablespoon
cornflour
60ml/4 tablespoons cold
water
4 green olives, sliced

1. Place the noodles in a bowl and pour on 150ml/¼ pint boiling water. Add salt. Cover with a lid or pierced cling film and cook on HIGH for 3 minutes.
2. Cover with foil and leave to stand for 3 minutes.
3. Place mushrooms in a bowl with the bay leaf, bouquet garni and 75ml/3floz boiling water. Cover and microwave on HIGH for 2 minutes.
4. Discard the bay leaf and bouquet garni. Blend the skimmed milk powder with the cornflour and cold water. Stir into the mushrooms.
5. Microwave on HIGH until boiling and thickened — about 1½ minutes, stirring briskly every 30 seconds.
6. Stir in the olives. Season to taste with salt and pepper.
7. Drain the noodles and serve the sauce on top.

Serving Suggestion:
A complete meal on its own.

NUTS AND VEGETABLE RISOTTO

Serves 1/415 calories

50g/2oz long-grain white
rice
1.25ml/¼ level teaspoon
dried mixed herbs
½ chicken stock cube
200ml/7floz boiling water
1 or 2 spring onions,
leaves discarded, sliced
1 tomato, chopped
50g/2oz frozen peas
25g/1oz mushrooms, sliced
25g/1oz roasted cashew
nuts or peanuts
Black pepper

1. Mix the rice and herbs in a deep bowl. Dissolve the stock cube in the boiling water and pour over the rice. Cover with a lid or pierced cling film and microwave on HIGH for 6 minutes.
2. Cover and leave to stand while you prepare the vegetables.
3. Place the spring onions, tomato and peas in a bowl. Cover and microwave on HIGH for 1½ minutes.
4. Add to the rice with the mushrooms. Cover and microwave on HIGH for 3 minutes.
5. Stir in the nuts and season with pepper. Cover and leave to stand until all the stock is absorbed.

Serving Suggestion:
A vegetarian main meal that is complete on its own.

BEANS IN CHILLI SAUCE

Serves 2/170 calories per portion

50g/2oz onion, chopped
1 clove garlic, crushed
227g/8oz can tomatoes
115g/4oz red pepper, deseeded and diced
5ml/1 level teaspoon chilli powder, hot or mild
1.25ml/¼ level teaspoon ground cumin
1.25ml/¼ level teaspoon ground coriander
5ml/1 level teaspoon brown sugar
425g/15oz can red kidney beans, drained
5ml/1 level teaspoon cornflour
Salt and pepper

1. Place the onion and garlic in a bowl.
2. Drain tomatoes and reserve the juice. Add 15ml/1 tablespoon juice to the onion and garlic. Cover with a lid or pierced cling film and microwave on HIGH for 2 minutes.
3. Chop the tomatoes and add to the bowl with the remaining juice. Add red pepper, chilli powder, cumin, coriander and sugar. Stir well, then cover and microwave on HIGH for 2 minutes.
4. Stir in the beans. Cover and microwave on HIGH for 1 minute.
5. Blend the cornflour with 45ml/3 tablespoons cold water. Stir into the beans. Cook on HIGH until the sauce boils and thickens, stirring briskly every 30 seconds. Season to taste.

Serving Suggestion:
Add some lightly boiled bean sprouts — a 115g/4oz helping looks a lot and costs just 30 calories.

LEEKS IN HERBY CHEESE SAUCE

Serves 1/405 calories

225g/8oz leeks, weighed trimmed, sliced thickly
30ml/2 tablespoons water
115ml/4floz skimmed milk
15ml/1 level tablespoon cornflour
50g/2oz Sage Derby cheese or Cheddar cheese with herbs, grated
Salt, pepper and mustard
30ml/2 level tablespoons fresh wholemeal breadcrumbs

1. Place the leeks in a dish with the water. Cover with a lid or pierced cling film and microwave on HIGH for 5 minutes, stirring twice.
2. Drain and add the water to the milk.
3. Blend the cornflour with a little of the milk until smooth. Heat the remaining milk on HIGH for 1 minute. Stir in the cornflour mixture and microwave on HIGH until it boils and thickens, stirring well every 30 seconds.
4. Add most of the cheese to the sauce. Season to taste with salt, pepper and mustard. Pour over the leeks.
5. Sprinkle the remaining cheese and the crumbs on top and grill until brown.

Serving Suggestion:
Eat on its own as a vegetarian main meal.

SPINACH AND CHEESE CUSTARD

Serves 1/300 calories

115g/4oz frozen chopped spinach
115ml/4floz skimmed milk
1 egg, size 3, beaten
25g/1oz mature Cheddar cheese, grated
15ml/1 level tablespoon grated Parmesan cheese
1 spring onion, leaves discarded, sliced
Pinch grated nutmeg
Salt and pepper

1. Place the frozen spinach in a dish. Cover with a lid or pierced cling film and microwave on DEFROST for 6 minutes.
2. Place in a sieve and press lightly with the back of a spoon to remove excess liquid.
3. Place milk in a jug and microwave on HIGH until hot but not boiling — about 1 minute.
4. Whisk the egg into the milk.
5. Stir the Cheddar cheese into the custard with the Parmesan, spinach, spring onion and nutmeg. Season to taste with salt and pepper.
6. Pour mixture into a dish, about 6 inches wide, then stand this dish in a larger one. Pour in enough boiling water into the larger dish to come up as far as the custard.
7. Microwave on HIGH for 4½ minutes. Leave to stand for 5 minutes.

Serving Suggestion:
Can be eaten hot or cold. Add some green salad vegetables if you wish.

PARSNIP AND POTATO BAKE

Serves 1/365 calories

150g/5oz parsnips, peeled weight, cored
60ml/4 tablespoons water
150g/5oz potatoes, peeled weight, diced
115g/4oz skimmed milk soft cheese
Salt and pepper
25g/1oz Edam cheese, grated

1. Place the parsnips in a dish with 30ml/2 tablespoons water. Cover with a lid or pierced cling film and microwave on HIGH for 5½ minutes.
2. Place the potatoes in a dish with 30ml/2 tablespoons water. Cover and microwave on HIGH for 5 minutes. Leave to stand for 4 minutes.
3. Drain both vegetables and mash with the skimmed milk cheese. Season to taste with salt and pepper.
4. Turn into a dish. Level the top. Sprinkle with the Edam cheese. Microwave on HIGH for 2 minutes.

Serving Suggestion:
Serve with a helping of boiled French beans if you wish — 115g/4oz weighed frozen costs 40 calories.

SPINACH PUDDING

Serves 2/285 calories per portion

1.25ml/¼ level teaspoon butter or margarine
450g/1lb frozen chopped spinach
75g/3oz fresh wholemeal breadcrumbs
2.5ml/½ level teaspoon fresh grated nutmeg
Grated rind of small lemon
50g/2oz curd cheese
2 eggs, size 3
Salt and pepper

1. Grease a 850ml/1½ pint pudding basin with the butter or margarine.
2. Place the spinach in a bowl and cover with pierced cling film. Cook on DEFROST until thawed — about 13 minutes. Then cook on HIGH for 1 minute.
3. Drain spinach in a sieve and press lightly with the back of a spoon to remove excess liquid.
4. Mix the spinach with the breadcrumbs, nutmeg and lemon rind.
5. Place the curd cheese in a bowl and microwave on DEFROST for 1 minute to soften.
6. Add cheese to the spinach with the beaten eggs. Season to taste with salt and pepper.
7. Turn mixture into the prepared basin. Cover with pierced cling film and microwave on HIGH for 3 minutes. Half turn the basin and cook on HIGH for a further 2 minutes. Leave to stand for 5 minutes. Then turn out.

Serving Suggestion:
This pudding should be served hot and makes a light meal to serve two people.

RED CABBAGE WITH APPLE

Serves 4/75 calories per portion

450g/1lb red cabbage, shredded
1 medium cooking apple, peeled, cored and diced
15ml/1 level tablepoon soft brown sugar
15ml/1 tablespoon lemon juice
15ml/1 tablespoon water
25g/1oz sultanas
Salt and pepper

1. Mix the cabbage, apple, sugar, lemon juice and water in a dish. Season lightly with salt and pepper. Cover with a lid or pierced cling film. Microwave on HIGH for 3 minutes.
2. Stir, cover again and microwave on HIGH for a further 3 minutes.
3. Stir in the sultanas, cover and microwave on HIGH for a further 6 minutes, stirring after 3 minutes.
4. Cover with foil and leave to stand for 10 minutes. Serve.

Serving Suggestion:
Try with a well-grilled pork chop — delicious.

STUFFED PEPPERS

Serves 2/260 calories per portion

2 medium-sized red or
green peppers
60ml/4 tablespoons water
40g/1½oz long-grain white
rice
200ml/7floz boiling water
1.25ml/¼ level teaspoon
ground coriander
1.25ml/¼ level teaspoon
ground cumin
2.5ml/½ level teaspoon
curry powder
25g/1oz onion, chopped
½ clove garlic, crushed
5ml/1 teaspoon oil
50g/2oz frozen peas
25g/1oz pine nuts
25g/1oz currants
Salt and pepper

1. Cut a slice from the top of each pepper and carefully scoop out the seeds and pith, using a teaspoon.
2. Place the empty peppers in a dish with their lids and 45ml/3 tablespoons water. Cover with a lid or pierced cling film and microwave on HIGH for 4 minutes. Turn the peppers round after 2 minutes.
3. Place the rice in a bowl with the boiling water. Cover and microwave on HIGH for 6 minutes. Leave to stand while preparing the other ingredients.
4. Place the onion and garlic in a bowl with 15ml/1 tablespoon water and the oil. Cover and microwave on HIGH for 2 minutes.
5. Stir in the coriander, cumin and curry powder. Add the peas. Cover and microwave on HIGH for a further 2 minutes.
6. Add the pine nuts and currants. Cover and microwave on HIGH for a further minute.
7. Drain off and discard any liquid from the rice. Add rice to the spice mixture and stir well.
8. Fill into the pepper cases and replace the lids. Cover and microwave on HIGH for 3 minutes.

Serving Suggestion:
A light meal to share to which you won't need to add anything.

PUMPKIN PURÉE

Serves 2/40 calories per portion

225g/8oz pumpkin, peeled
weight, cubed
30ml/2 tablespoons water
25g/1oz skimmed milk soft
cheese
Pinch grated nutmeg
Salt and pepper

1. Place pumpkin in a dish. Cover with a lid or pierced cling film. Microwave on HIGH for 4 minutes.
2. Rearrange the pieces, cover again and microwave for a further 3 minutes. Leave to stand for 3 minutes.
3. Drain, then mash with the nutmeg and skimmed milk soft cheese. Season to taste with salt and pepper.

Serving Suggestion:
Pumpkin's slightly sweet taste makes it a good accompaniment to pork or chicken.

STIR-FRIED WATER CHESTNUTS AND CASHEW NUTS

Serves 1/315 calories

5ml/1 teaspoon
Sharwood's oyster sauce
5ml/1 teaspoon soy sauce
5ml/1 teaspoon honey
5ml/1 teaspoon cider
vinegar or wine vinegar
60ml/4 tablespoons orange
juice
5ml/1 level teaspoon
cornflour
Salt and pepper
5ml/1 teaspoon oil
5ml/1 level teaspoon
grated root ginger
1 stick celery, thinly sliced
25g/1oz whole green
beans, fresh or frozen,
halved
25g/1oz red pepper, cut
into matchsticks
25g/1oz green pepper, cut
into matchsticks
1 spring onion, leaves
discarded, thinly sliced
50g/2oz water chestnuts,
thinly sliced
25g/1oz roasted cashew
nuts

1. Mix together the oyster sauce, soy sauce, honey, vinegar, orange juice and cornflour. Season to taste with salt and pepper.
2. Place the oil and ginger in a shallow dish and microwave on HIGH for 20 seconds.
3. Add the celery and beans and stir to mix. Microwave on HIGH for 2 minutes.
4. Stir in the peppers, spring onion and water chestnuts. Microwave on HIGH for 1 minute.
5. Stir in the cashew nuts and sauce mixture. Microwave on HIGH for a further 1½ minutes, stirring briskly every 30 seconds until boiling and thickened. Serve.

Serving Suggestion:
There is no need to add anything more to this tasty vegetarian meal.

CHICORY WITH ORANGE

Serves 1/45 calories

2 chicory heads, halved
lengthwise
30ml/2 tablespoons
unsweetened orange juice
5ml/1 level teaspoon low-
fat spread
Salt and pepper (optional)
Little chopped parsley

1. Place chicory in a dish in a single layer and spoon over the orange juice.
2. Dot with low-fat spread. Cover with a lid or pierced cling film. Microwave on HIGH for 3 minutes. Leave to stand for 2 minutes.
3. Sprinkle with parsley and serve.

Serving Suggestion:
Chicory is just 3 calories per raw 28g/1oz and is most often used in cold salads. But try chicory this way served with chicken or lamb kebabs.

RUNNER BEANS NICOISE

Serves 2/45 calories per portion

225g/8oz runner beans, thickly sliced
30ml/4 tablespoons water
227g/8oz can tomatoes
1 small clove garlic, crushed
2 spring onions, leaves discarded, thinly sliced
Pinch dried basil or oregano
2.5ml/½ level teaspoon sugar
Salt and pepper

1. Place runner beans in a serving dish with the water and cover with a lid or pierced cling film. Microwave on HIGH for 3 minutes. Stir, cover again and microwave for a further 3 minutes. Leave to stand, covered with foil, shiny side down.
2. Drain the tomatoes and reserve 60ml/4 tablespoons juice. Chop the tomatoes. Place with reserved juice in a dish and add garlic, spring onions, herbs and sugar. Cover and microwave on HIGH for 1½ minutes.
3. Stir, cover again, and microwave for a further 1½ minutes.
4. Drain beans. Pour sauce over the beans and serve.

Serving Suggestion:
Good with white fish, either cooked in the microwave or grilled with the minimum of fat.

COURGETTES AU GRATIN

Serves 1/185 calories

115g/4oz courgettes, thinly sliced
115g/4oz tomatoes, peeled and sliced
1 spring onion, leaves discarded, thinly sliced
½ small clove garlic, crushed (optional)
5ml/1 level teaspoon chopped parsley
Pinch dried basil or
2.5ml/½ level teaspoon chopped fresh basil
Pepper
25g/1oz mature Cheddar cheese, grated
15g/½oz fresh wholemeal breadcrumbs

1. Place the courgettes, tomatoes, spring onion, garlic, parsley and basil in a dish. Season with pepper and mix well.
2. Cover with a lid or pierced cling film and microwave on HIGH for 3 minutes.
3. Stir, cover again and microwave on HIGH for a further 3 minutes.
4. Stir, cover and microwave on HIGH for a further 2 minutes.
5. Mix the cheese with the breadcrumbs. Sprinkle on top of courgettes and grill until brown.

Serving Suggestion:
Eat with some crispy French bread — 85 calories per 28g/1oz — to make a light meal.

CHEESE AND TOMATO SCONE PIZZA

Serves 4/255 calories per portion

115g/4oz plain wholemeal flour
10ml/2 level teaspoons baking powder
Salt and pepper
25g/1oz butter or margarine
75ml/5 tablespoons skimmed milk
227g/8oz can tomatoes
3 spring onions, leaves discarded, sliced
10ml/2 level teaspoons chopped fresh basil or oregano or 1.25ml/¼ level teaspoon dried basil or oregano
75g/3oz mature Cheddar cheese, grated
8 black or green olives, stoned

1. Mix the flour with the baking powder and a pinch of salt. Rub in the butter or margarine. Mix with enough milk to make a soft but not sticky dough.
2. Place on a piece of greaseproof paper and pat out into an 8-9 inch round. Place on a plate and microwave on HIGH for 4 minutes. Remove the paper.
3. Drain the tomatoes thoroughly and discard the juice (or save to add to a casserole). Chop the tomatoes and mix with the spring onions and herbs.
4. Spread tomato mixture on the scone base and season with pepper.
5. Sprinkle the cheese over the tomatoes and arrange olives on top. Microwave on HIGH for 3 minutes.

Serving Suggestion:
Makes a tasty lunch to share with family or friends. Serve with crisp green salad.

STUFFED TOMATOES

Serves 2/130 calories per portion

2 large tomatoes, 115g/4oz each
25g/1oz mature Cheddar cheese, grated
40g/1½oz canned sweetcorn, drained
25g/1oz fresh wholemeal breadcrumbs
5ml/1 level teaspoon chopped parsley
5ml/1 level teaspoon low calorie salad dressing
5ml/1 level teaspoon chopped chives or pinch dried chives
Salt and pepper

1. Cut a slice off the top of the tomatoes and scoop out the insides with a teaspoon. Discard the hard core and reserve the rest.
2. Mix the cheese with the sweetcorn, breadcrumbs, parsley, chives and low calorie salad dressing.
3. Add the reserved tomato pulp and season with salt and pepper. Spoon back into the tomato cases and replace the lids.
4. Microwave on HIGH for 1½ minutes. Rearrange and cook for a further 2 minutes. Leave to stand for 1½ minutes.

Serving Suggestion:
Ideal accompaniment to a grill. You could also serve two stuffed tomatoes as a light lunch.

MICROWAVE MAIN MEAL
Beef in Oyster Sauce

**MICROWAVE MAIN
MEALS**
Neptune's Plaice; Kidney
Provencale; Pork Fillet w
Cumbrian Sauce; Persian
Stuffed Chicken

BUTTER BEAN CURRY

Serves 1/235 calories

25g/1oz onion, chopped
2.5ml/½ level teaspoon grated root ginger
5ml/1 level teaspoon oil
2.5ml/½ level teaspoon ground cumin
2.5ml/½ level teaspoon ground coriander
1.25ml/¼ level teaspoon chilli powder, hot or mild
2.5ml/½ level teaspoon ground turmeric
25g/1oz green pepper, cut into strips
1 medium tomato, peeled and chopped
15ml/1 level tablespoon sultanas
227g/8oz can butter beans
10ml/2 level teaspoons cornflour
Salt and pepper

1. Place the onion in a dish with the ginger and oil. Stir to mix. Cover with a lid or pierced cling film and microwave on HIGH for 2 minutes.
2. Stir in the cumin, coriander, chilli powder and turmeric. Cover and microwave on HIGH for 1 minute.
3. Drain the beans and reserve 60ml/4 tablespoons liquid. Add 30ml/2 tablespoons to the dish.
4. Stir the pepper, tomato and sultanas into the spicy mixture. Cover and cook on HIGH for 1½ minutes.
5. Add the drained beans. Cover and cook on HIGH for a further minute.
6. Blend the cornflour with the remaining 30ml/2 tablespoons liquid and stir in.
7. Microwave on HIGH for 2½ minutes, stirring every 30 seconds. Season to taste.

Serving Suggestion:
If you add a 75g/3oz helping boiled brown rice (28g/1oz weighed dry) count 100 calories extra. A few lightly boiled bean sprouts mixed with the rice adds crunch and bulk for 7 calories per 28g/1oz.

PEPPERONATA

Serves 1/45 calories

25g/1oz onion, chopped
½ clove garlic, crushed
50g/2oz canned chopped tomatoes, drained weight
30ml/2 tablespoons tomato juice from can
50g/2oz red pepper, cut into strips
50g/2oz green pepper, cut into strips
2.5ml/½ level teaspoon sugar
1.25ml/¼ level teaspoon dried basil
Salt and pepper

1. Place onion and garlic in a dish with 15ml/1 tablespoon tomato juice. Cover with a lid or pierced cling film and microwave on HIGH for 1 minute.
2. Add the tomatoes to the dish with the remaining juice.
3. Add peppers with the sugar and basil. Season with salt and pepper to taste.
4. Cover and microwave on HIGH for 3 minutes. Leave to stand for 3 minutes.

Serving Suggestion:
With meat or fish or serve as a sauce for pasta.

RATATOUILLE

Serves 4/65 calories per portion

225g/8oz aubergine, cubed
Salt and pepper
75g/3oz onion, chopped
1 clove garlic, crushed
15ml/1 tablespoon oil
227g/8oz can tomatoes
40g/1½oz red pepper, cut into strips
40g/1½oz yellow or green pepper, cut into strips
225g/8oz courgettes, thinly sliced
5ml/1 level teaspoon tomato purée

1. Sprinkle aubergine with salt and leave to stand for 30 minutes. Rinse with cold water and pat dry with kitchen paper.
2. Place the onion and garlic in a bowl with the oil. Cover with a lid or pierced cling film and microwave on HIGH for 2 minutes.
3. Drain the tomatoes and reserve 30ml/2 tablespoons juice. Place the peppers, courgettes, aubergine and tomato juice in the bowl. Stir well. Cover and mircrowave on HIGH for 4 minutes. Stir well, cover again and microwave on HIGH for a further 4 minutes.
4. Chop the tomatoes and stir in with the tomato purée. Cover and microwave on HIGH for 4 minutes. Leave to stand for 5 minutes. Season with salt and pepper to taste.

Serving Suggestion:
A very useful vegetable mixture which will freeze in individual portions if you aren't serving four people. A double portion with a little cheese makes a light meal on its own.

LEEKS IN TOMATO SAUCE

Serves 1/120 calories

175g/6oz white part of leeks, weighed trimmed, sliced thickly
175g/6oz tomatoes, skinned and chopped
1 spring onion, leaves discarded, chopped
2.5ml/½ level teaspoon sugar
1.25ml/¼ level teaspoon dried mixed herbs
15ml/1 tablespoon water
Salt and pepper
15ml/1 level tablespoon grated Parmesan cheese

1. Mix together all the ingredients except the Parmesan cheese and leeks, in a wide-based dish. Season with salt and pepper.
2. Cover with a lid or pierced cling film and microwave on HIGH for 5 minutes, stirring twice. This should make a thick sauce; if necessary leave the cover off and cook for a further minute to allow any excess liquid to evaporate.
3. Stir in the leeks. Cover and microwave on HIGH for 3 minutes.
4. Stir, cover again and microwave on HIGH for a further 3 minutes. Leave to stand for 2 minutes.
5. Sprinkle with Parmesan cheese and serve.

Serving Suggestion:
Particularly good with chicken, turkey or white fish.

CABBAGE WITH CARAWAY

Serves 4/50 calories per portion

450g/1lb white cabbage, shredded
5ml/1 level teaspoon caraway seeds
30ml/2 tablespoons water
30ml/2 level tablespoons soured cream
75ml/5 level tablespoons low-fat natural yogurt
Salt and pepper

1. Mix the cabbage with the caraway seeds. Place in a dish with the water. Cover with a lid or pierced cling film and microwave on HIGH for 7 minutes, stirring every 2½ minutes.
2. Drain off any excess liquid. Stir in the yogurt and soured cream. Cover and microwave on HIGH for 1 minute.
3. Season to taste with salt and pepper. Cover with foil and leave to stand for 5 minutes.

Serving Suggestion:
A creamy-tasting vegetable dish which is delicious with roast beef. Remember to discard any visible fat from the beef and you'll save lots of calories.

CAULIFLOWER IN CUMIN SAUCE

Serves 1/175 calories

175g/6oz cauliflower florets
60ml/4 tablespoons water
5ml/1 level teaspoon butter
5ml/1 level teaspoon ground cumin
150ml/¼ pint skimmed milk
15ml/1 level tablespoon cornflour
Salt and pepper
15ml/1 level tablespoon flaked almonds

1. Place the cauliflower in a serving dish. Add water and cover with a lid or pierced cling film. Microwave on HIGH for 4½ minutes.
2. Cover with foil and leave to stand while you make the sauce.
3. Place the butter in a jug or bowl and microwave on HIGH for 20 seconds.
4. Stir in the cumin and microwave on HIGH for 30 seconds.
5. Stir in 115ml/4floz milk and microwave on HIGH for 1½ minutes.
6. Blend the cornflour with remaining milk and stir into sauce. Stir well, then microwave on HIGH until it thickens and bubbles, whisking every 20 seconds. Season to taste with salt and pepper.
7. Drain the cauliflower and pour the sauce on top.
8. Sprinkle the almonds on a plate and microwave on HIGH for 1½ minutes. Sprinkle on the cauliflower and serve.

Serving Suggestion:
Particularly nice with microwaved or grilled trout.

STIR-FRIED BEAN SPROUTS AND VEGETABLES

Serves 1/80 calories

5ml/1 teaspoon oil
5ml/1 teaspoon grated
root ginger
25g/1oz carrot, cut into
matchsticks
50g/2oz button
mushrooms, thinly sliced
25g/1oz red pepper, cut
into matchsticks
1 spring onion, leaves
discarded, thinly sliced
50g/2oz bean sprouts
5ml/1 teaspoon soy sauce
Salt and pepper

1. Place the oil and ginger in a shallow dish and microwave on HIGH for 20 seconds.
2. Stir in the carrots and microwave on HIGH for 1 minute.
3. Stir in the mushrooms, pepper, spring onion and bean sprouts. Microwave on HIGH for a further minute.
4. Stir and microwave on HIGH for a further minute.
5. Stir in the soy sauce and season to taste with salt and pepper.

Serving Suggestion:
Gives a Chinese flavour to cooked chicken or turkey.

BAKED POTATO WITH YOGURT

Serves 1/180 calories

1 potato, 225g/8oz
15ml/1 level tablespoon
low-fat natural yogurt
2.5ml-5ml/½-1 level
teaspoon chopped chives
or pinch of dried chives

1. Scrub the potato and prick on both sides with a fork. Place on a double thickness piece of kitchen paper and microwave on HIGH for 3½ minutes.
2. Turn potato over and reposition slightly. Cook on HIGH for a further 3½ minutes. Leave to stand for 3 minutes.
3. Cut a cross in the top of the potato and squeeze gently to open. Mix the yogurt with the chives and spoon on top.

Serving Suggestion:
Can be served as an accompaniment to meat or fish if you have the calories to spare. Will also make a vegetarian meal served with beans or salad.

FRENCH-STYLE PEAS

Serves 1/90 calories

115g/4oz frozen peas
2 or 3 spring onions,
leaves discarded, thinly
sliced
2 leaves lettuce, shredded
1 fresh mint leaf, chopped
15ml/1 tablespoon water
1.25ml/¼ level teaspoon
caster sugar
5ml/1 level teaspoon low-
fat spread
Salt and pepper

1. Place the peas in a dish.
2. Add the spring onions, lettuce, mint and water to the peas. Cover with a lid or pierced cling film and microwave on HIGH for 4 minutes.
3. Stir in the sugar and low-fat spread and season to taste with salt and pepper.

Serving Suggestion:
Makes peas extra special and very good with plain grilled fish.

SWEDE AND POTATO PURÉE

Serves 2/105 calories

115g/4oz swede, weighed
peeled, cubed
60ml/4 tablespoons water
115g/4oz potato, weighed
peeled, cubed
115g/4oz skimmed milk
soft cheese
Salt and pepper

1. Place swede in a dish with 30ml/2 tablespoons water. Cover with a lid or pierced cling film and microwave on HIGH for 5 minutes.
2. Place the potato in a dish with 30ml/2 tablespoons water. Cover and microwave on HIGH for 4 minutes. Leave to stand for 3 minutes.
3. Drain both vegetables and mash with skimmed milk soft cheese. Season to taste with salt and pepper and place in a serving dish.
4. Reheat on HIGH for 1 minute.

Serving Suggestion:
Serve with any roast or microwaved meat dish.

Vegetables can be microwaved in a covered container with a small quantity of water. When you cook a jacket potato, wrap it in kitchen paper. Here are some basic fresh vegetables which you may like to serve with any of the main or light meals in this book. Timings are for a 600 watt microwave.

VEGETABLE	PORTION	CALORIES	COOKING TIMES (MINUTES)
Broad beans	115g/4oz	135	2½-3½
French beans	115g/4oz	40	3½-4
Runner beans	115g/4oz	30	3½-4½
Broccoli	115g/4oz	30	2½-3
Brussels sprouts	115g/4oz	30	3½-4
Cabbage	115g/4oz	25	3½-4½
Cauliflower	115g/4oz	15	3-4
Carrots	115g/4oz	25	2½-3½
Courgettes	115g/4oz	15	2½-3½
Mushrooms	115g/4oz	15	2-2½
Leeks (sliced)	115g/4oz	35	2½-3
Mangetout	75g/3oz	50	2½-3
Potatoes (new)	175g/6oz	125	2-3
Potatoes (jacket)	175g/6oz	130	5-6
Peas	115g/4oz	75	2½-3½
Spinach	115g/4oz	30	2-2½
Swede	115g/4oz	25	3-4
Corn on the Cob	215g/7½oz	125	4-5

SPEEDY PUDDINGS

A microwave is ideal for cooking small quantities of fruit and you'll find here recipes for poached peaches and pears, stewed and baked apples and baked banana. But you can also use your microwave to make fools, custards, bread pudding, meringues and mousses. Recipes serve either one, two or four and none costs more than 250 calories a portion. In fact, there are many recipes that add up to under 100 calories: they'd cheaply satisfy a sweet craving at any time.

CHERRIES IN YOGURT CUSTARD

Serves 2/185 calories per portion

225g/8oz eating cherries, stoned
15ml/1 tablespoon apple juice
1 egg yolk
15g/½oz custard powder
150ml/¼ pint low-fat natural yogurt
15ml/1 level tablespoon fruit sugar (fructose)
1 or 2 drops vanilla essence
15ml/1 level tablespoon flaked almonds

1. Place the cherries in a dish with the apple juice. Cover with a lid or pierced cling film and microwave on DEFROST for 6 minutes until tender.
2. Drain off all the juice.
3. Whisk together the egg yolk, custard powder, yogurt, fruit sugar and vanilla essence. Pour over the cherries.
4. Microwave on HIGH for 1 minute and then on DEFROST for 4 minutes. Shake dish and tilt carefully so that some runny mixture from the centre goes to the edge. Microwave on DEFROST for a further 4 minutes. Leave to stand 10 minutes.
5. Sprinkle the almonds on a plate and microwave on HIGH for 1½ minutes. Sprinkle over custard before serving.

PLUM AND PEACH MERINGUE

Serves 2/140 calories per portion

225g/8oz dessert plums, halved, stoned and sliced
30ml/2 tablespoons water
1 medium peach, 175g/6oz, peeled, halved, stoned and sliced
5ml/1 level teaspoon honey
1 egg white
25g/1oz caster sugar

1. Place the plums in a large dish with the water. Cover with a lid or pierced cling film and microwave on HIGH for 1½ minutes.
2. Stir peach slices into the plums with the honey. The dish should be less than half full as the meringue expands when cooked.
3. Whisk the egg white until stiff. Add half the sugar and whisk until stiff again. Gently fold in the remaining sugar.
4. Spread the meringue over the top of the fruit, making sure that it goes right to the edges of the dish. Microwave on HIGH for 2 minutes until the meringue is firm. Brown lightly under the grill if desired. Serve hot or cold.

BAKED EGG CUSTARD

Serves 1/135 calories

115ml/4floz skimmed milk
1 egg, size 3
5ml/1 level teaspoon
caster sugar
Few drops vanilla essence
Pinch grated nutmeg

1. Place milk in a jug and microwave on HIGH for 1 minute. Do not boil.
2. Place egg, sugar and vanilla essence in a bowl which will hold at least 575ml/1 pint. Whisk until well blended then whisk in the hot milk. Sprinkle the nutmeg on top.
3. Stand the bowl in a fairly shallow dish and pour in enough boiling water to come level with the custard.
4. Microwave on HIGH for 4-5 minutes or until just set in the centre. Do not overcook. The exact cooking time will vary with the depth of the custard. Leave to stand for 5 minutes.
5. Remove bowl from the dish and serve warm or leave to cool.

NECTARINES IN STRAWBERRY SAUCE

Serves 4/115 calories per portion

4 medium-sized nectarines
175g/6oz each
60ml/4 tablespoons orange juice
225g/8oz strawberries, fresh, hulled or frozen, thawed
20ml/4 level teaspoons icing sugar

1. Plunge the nectarines into a bowl of boiling water for 1 minute, then into a bowl of cold water for 1 minute. Peel (the skin should come off easily now) then place nectarines in a dish leaving a gap between them.
2. Pour over the orange juice. Cover with a lid or pierced cling film and cook on HIGH for 2 minutes.
3. Turn over and reposition slightly. Cover and cook on HIGH for a further 2 minutes. Leave to cool.
4. Drain off the juice and pour it into a blender or food processor. Add the strawberries and icing sugar. Blend until smooth.
5. Pour strawberry sauce over the nectarines. Cover and chill.

POACHED PEAR IN BLACKCURRANT SAUCE

Serves 1/110 calories

1 pear, 150g/5oz, peeled, cored and quartered
30ml/2 tablespoons unsweetened apple juice
75g/3oz blackcurrants, fresh or frozen, thawed
10ml/2 level teaspoons caster sugar

1. Place the pear in a dish with the apple juice. Cover with a lid or pierced cling film and microwave on HIGH for 1½ minutes.
2. Lift out the pear and place in a serving dish.
3. Add the blackcurrants and sugar to the juice in the dish. Cover and microwave on HIGH for 1 minute or until tender. Push through a nylon sieve and pour over the pears. Chill before serving.

STEWED APPLE WITH RAISINS

Serves 1/95 calories

115g/4oz cooking apple, peeled weight, cored and thinly sliced
15ml/1 tablespoon apple juice
5ml/1 level teaspoon honey
15ml/1 level tablespoon raisins or sultanas
Pinch ground cinnamon (optional)

1. Place the apples, apple juice, honey and raisins or sultanas in a bowl. Add the cinnamon if used. Cover with a lid or pierced cling film and microwave on HIGH for 2 minutes. Stir gently.
2. Cover again and microwave on HIGH for 2-3 minutes or until the apples are soft. Leave to stand for 2 minutes. Serve hot or cold.

PEAR WITH GINGER STUFFING

Serves 1/130 calories

1 ginger biscuit
25g/1oz skimmed milk soft cheese
1 pear, 175g/6oz, peeled, halved and cored
15ml/1 tablespoon apple juice

1. Crush the biscuit and mix with the cheese.
2. Place pear halves in a dish, hollow side up and fill with the ginger mixture. Pour the apple juice around the dish.
3. Cover with a lid or pierced cling film and microwave on HIGH for 1 minute.

Variation:
PEAR WITH CHOCOLATE SAUCE
Replace the gingernut and cheese with a crushed chocolate digestive biscuit and 2 chopped glacé cherries. Cook on HIGH for 1¼ minutes.

GUAVA CREAM

Serves 2/130 calories per portion

10ml/2 level teaspoons
powdered gelatine
30ml/2 tablespoons water
283g/10oz can guavas in
natural juice
115ml/4floz unsweetened
orange juice
25g/1oz skimmed milk
powder
1 egg white

1. Sprinkle the gelatine onto the water in a small basin or cup. Leave to soak for 5 minutes.
2. Add 60ml/4 tablespoons orange juice and microwave on HIGH for 1-2 minutes until dissolved. Add the remaining juice.
3. Place the guavas and their juice in a blender or food processor with the powdered milk. Purée until smooth. Add the gelatine mixture and chill until on the point of setting.
4. Whisk the egg white and fold in. Divide between two glasses and chill until set.

TIPSY CHERRIES

Serves 1/110 calories

115g/4oz dessert cherries
15ml/1 tablespoon sweet
vermouth or port
10ml/2 level teaspoons
cherry jam
15ml/1 tablespoon orange
juice

1. Place all the ingredients in a serving dish. Cover with a lid or pierced cling film and microwave on HIGH for 1 minute.
2. Stir and then cover again. Microwave on HIGH for a further minute.
3. Leave to stand for 2 minutes. Serve hot or cold.

POACHED PEACH IN RASPBERRY SAUCE

Serves 1/90 calories

1 peach, 150g/5oz, peeled,
quartered and stoned
30ml/2 tablespoons
unsweetened orange juice
50g/2oz raspberries, fresh
or frozen, thawed
5ml/1 level teaspoon icing
sugar

1. Place peach in a dish with the orange juice. Cover with a lid or pierced cling film and microwave on HIGH for 1½ minutes. Leave to cool.
2. Press the raspberries through a nylon sieve and mix with the icing sugar and any juice from the peach. Pour over the peach and serve.

PEAR IN VERMOUTH

Serves 1/85 calories

1 medium pear, 150g/5oz
15ml/1 tablespoon sweet
vermouth
5ml/1 level teaspoon
caster sugar
2.5ml/½ teaspoon lemon
juice
45ml/3 tablespoons water

1. Peel the pear and place in a small dish.
2. Add all the other ingredients. Cover with a lid or pierced cling film and microwave on HIGH for 1½ minutes.
3. Turn over, cover again and microwave on HIGH for a further 1½ minutes.
4. Leave to stand for 3 minutes and serve hot or cold.

BAKED APPLE WITH SULTANAS

Serves 1/140 calories

1 cooking apple, 200g/7oz,
cored
30ml/2 level tablespoons
sultanas
5ml/1 level teaspoon
brown sugar
15ml/1 tablespoon apple
juice

1. Slit the skin around the centre of the apple. Stand in a small dish and fill with sultanas and sugar. Spoon over the apple juice.
2. Microwave on HIGH for 2½ minutes. Leave to stand for 2 minutes. Check, and if necessary, microwave on HIGH for a further ½-1 minute. Serve hot.

CARIBBEAN BANANA

Serves 1/150 calories

2.5ml/½ level teaspoon
butter
1 medium banana
10ml/2 teaspoons lime
cordial
10ml/2 teaspoons dark
rum
5ml/1 level teaspoon soft
brown sugar

1. Grease a small oval or oblong dish with the butter. Peel the banana and cut in half. Cut each piece in half lengthways. Arrange in the dish in a single layer.
2. Pour on the lime cordial and rum. Sprinkle with brown sugar. Microwave on HIGH for 45 seconds.
3. Rearrange the pieces of banana and baste with the juices. Cook on HIGH for a further 45 seconds. Serve immediately.

PINEAPPLE KIRSCH SORBET

Serves 4/130 calories per portion

**1 medium-sized pineapple
50g/2oz caster sugar
50ml/2floz water
15ml/1 tablespoon Kirsch
1 egg white**

1. Peel the pineapple and weigh 575g/1¼lb flesh. Cut flesh into chunks. Turn the freezer to fast freeze.
2. Place the sugar and water in a bowl and microwave on HIGH for 1½ minutes. Stir until sugar is completely melted, then leave to cool.
3. Purée the pineapple flesh in a blender or food processor, then add to the sugar syrup with the Kirsch.
4. Turn into a shallow container, cover and freeze until just firm.
5. Blend in a food processor until smooth.
6. Whisk the egg white until stiff and fold into sorbet. Return to the container, cover and freeze until hard.
7. Change the freezer control back to normal. To serve, microwave on DEFROST for 2 minutes then scoop into glasses.

RASPBERRY COBBLER

Serves 4/175 calories per portion

**450g/1lb raspberries, fresh
or frozen
45ml/3 level tablespoons
fruit sugar (fructose)
15ml/1 level tablespoon
cornflour
75g/3oz plain wholemeal
flour
7.5ml/1½ level teaspoons
baking powder
20g/¾oz butter or
margarine
45ml/3 tablespoons
skimmed milk**

1. Place the raspberries, 30ml/2 level tablespoons fruit sugar and the cornflour in a dish. Stir gently to mix. Cover with a lid or pierced cling film and microwave on HIGH for 4 minutes, if raspberries are fresh or 6 minutes if they are frozen. Stir every 2 minutes.
2. Mix flour, baking powder and 15ml/1 level tablespoon fruit sugar in a bowl. Rub in butter or margarine and then mix in milk. Pat into a 150cm/6 inch round and cut into four.
3. Place these wedges on top of the raspberries. Microwave on HIGH for 4 minutes. Serve warm.

APRICOT AND APPLE MOUSSE

Serves 4/175 calories per portion

**115g/4oz dried apricots
150ml/¼ pint apple juice
350g/12oz eating apples
(preferably Cox or Granny
Smith), peeled and cored
weight, sliced
15ml/1 level tablespoon
apricot jam
50g/2oz powdered
skimmed milk
115ml/4floz water
1 envelope powdered
gelatine, 10g
2 egg whites**

1. Place the apricots and apple juice in a large bowl. Cover with a lid or pierced cling film and microwave on HIGH for 5 minutes.
2. Add the apples to the dish. Stir, cover and microwave on HIGH for 5 minutes or until tender.
3. Purée in a blender or food processor with the apricot jam and skimmed milk powder. Turn into a measuring jug.
4. Place 45ml/3 tablespoons water in a small basin and sprinkle with the gelatine. Leave to soak for 5 minutes. Microwave on HIGH until dissolved — about 30 seconds. Stir into the purée and add extra water to make up to 575ml/1 pint.
5. Chill until on the point of setting. Whisk the egg whites until stiff and fold in gently. Turn into a dish and chill until set.

GREENGAGE FOOL

Serves 2/130 calories per portion

**225g/8oz greengages,
halved and stoned
15ml/1 tablespoon apple
juice
30ml/2 level tablespoons
fruit sugar (fructose)
115ml/4floz skimmed milk
15ml/1 level tablespoon
custard powder**

1. Place the greengages in a dish with the apple juice. Cover with a lid or pierced cling film and microwave on HIGH for 2½ minutes or until tender.
2. Stir in the sugar until dissolved. Purée in a blender or rub through a sieve.
3. Mix the milk and custard powder in a jug until smooth. Microwave on HIGH for 2 minutes until boiling and thickened, stirring briskly every 30 seconds. Cover the surface with damp greaseproof paper.
4. When the fruit purée and the custard have cooled, mix together. Divide between two glasses.

Variation:
**GOOSEBERRY FOOL
Substitute 225g/8oz
gooseberries for the
greengages. Calories per
portion: 100.**

SUMMER PUDDING

Serves 4/165 calories per portion

115g/4oz blackcurrants
115g/4oz redcurrants
60ml/4 tablespoons water
50g/2oz fruit sugar
(fructose)
115g/4oz raspberries
115g/4oz strawberries,
hulled
150g/5oz sliced, crustless
white bread

1. Place the blackcurrants, redcurrants and water in a bowl. Cover with a lid or pierced cling film and microwave on HIGH for 3 minutes, stirring after 1½ minutes.
2. Stir in the fruit sugar and raspberries. Cover and microwave on HIGH for 1 minute.
3. Quarter the strawberries if large or leave whole if small. Add to the hot fruit. Leave to cool.
4. Select a basin or soufflé dish which holds approximately 1½ pints. Cut 3 circles of bread to fit the bottom, middle and top. Cut the remaining bread to fit the sides of the basin.
5. Dip the pieces of bread in the juice and line the base and sides of the basin. Half fill with fruit and place the middle piece of bread on top. Fill with the remaining fruit and cover with the last circle of bread.
6. Cover with a piece of greaseproof paper and place a saucer on top — it should fit inside the basin. Place a 450g/1lb weight (or a can of the same weight) on the saucer and refrigerate overnight. Turn out to serve.

FIGS IN WINE AND HONEY

Serves 2/135 calories per portion

4 fresh figs, about
225g/8oz
150ml/¼ pint sweet white
wine
10ml/2 level teaspoons
honey

1. Wash and dry the figs.
2. Place the wine in a bowl and microwave on HIGH until boiling — about 4½ minutes. Stir in the honey.
3. Add the figs. Cover with a lid or pierced cling film and microwave on DEFROST for 5-6 minutes until tender. The exact cooking time will vary depending on the ripeness of the figs. Chill before serving.

COFFEE WALNUT CREAM

Serves 4/195 calories per portion

25g/1oz soft brown sugar
30ml/2 level tablespoons
plain flour
25g/1oz cornflour
425ml/¾ pint skimmed
milk
10ml/2 level teaspoons
instant coffee
3 egg yolks, size 3
2 egg whites, size 3
15g/½oz caster sugar
15g/½oz walnuts

1. Place the brown sugar, plain flour and cornflour, coffee and skimmed milk in a bowl. Whisk until well mixed. Microwave on HIGH for 6 minutes until thick, whisking well every 1½ minutes.
2. Lightly beat the yolks in a bowl. Gradually add 75ml/5 tablespoons hot custard, mixing well after each tablespoon. Whisk the yolks into the remaining custard.
3. Microwave on HIGH for 1 minute, whisking after 30 seconds. Cover the surface with damp greaseproof paper and leave to cool.
4. Whisk the egg whites until stiff. Add the caster sugar and whisk until stiff again. Fold into the custard. Divide between four glasses. Chop nuts and sprinkle on top.

RICE PUDDING WITH SULTANAS

Serves 4/160 calories per portion

50g/2oz round grain
(pudding) rice
575ml/1 pint semi-
skimmed milk
25g/1oz sugar
30ml/2 level tablespoons
sultanas

1. Place the rice, milk, sugar and sultanas in a large bowl. Cover with a lid or pierced cling film and microwave on HIGH for 5 minutes.
2. Stir well. Cover and microwave on DEFROST for 40 minutes, stirring well every 10 minutes.
3. Stir and cook on DEFROST, uncovered, for a further 5-10 minutes or until creamy. Leave to stand for 10 minutes. Serve hot or cold.

FREEZER SNACKS
Butter Bean and Tomato Stuffing
used to fill an Onion, Courgettes,
Squash and Pepper

FREEZER PATES AND SPREADS
Curried Butter Bean and Apple; Blue
Cheese and Walnut; Skippers Pâté;
Corned Beef and Horseradish
Spread

STUFFED PEACH

Serves 2/145 calories per portion

2 large peaches, 175g/6oz each, peeled, halved and stoned
1 sponge finger biscuit, crushed
1 large digestive biscuit, crushed
15ml/1 level tablespoon ground almonds
20ml/4 teaspoons apple juice
15ml/1 level tablespoon flaked almonds

1. Arrange peach halves around the edge of a dish, hollow side up.
2. Mix together the crushed sponge finger and digestive biscuit, ground almonds and apple juice. Spoon into the stone cavities. Press the flaked almonds into the stuffing.
3. Cover with a lid or pierced cling film. Microwave on HIGH for 1½ minutes. Turn the peaches around so that the inside edges go to the outside. Cover and microwave for a further minute. Leave to stand for 2 minutes. Serve hot.

RHUBARB AND ORANGE FLUFF

Serves 4/90 calories per portion

350g/12oz rhubarb, cut into short lengths
115ml/4floz boiling water
1 packet sugar-free orange jelly
2 medium bananas, peeled and quartered
25g/1oz powdered skimmed milk
2 egg whites

1. Place the rhubarb and boiling water in a dish. Cover with a lid or pierced cling film and microwave on HIGH until tender — about 6 minutes, but the exact time will depend on the age of the rhubarb.
2. Add jelly to the dish and stir until dissolved. Leave to cool.
3. Place in a blender or food processor with the skimmed milk powder and banana. Blend until smooth.
4. Chill until on the point of setting. Whisk the egg whites until stiff and fold in gently. Divide between four dishes and chill until set.

APPLE AND BLACKBERRY MERINGUE

Serves 4/180 calories per portion

350g/12oz cooking apples, peeled and cored weight, sliced
350g/12oz blackberries
30ml/2 level tablespoons honey
2 egg whites
Pinch cream of tartar
75g/3oz caster sugar

1. Place the apples and blackberries in a dish with the honey. Cover with a lid or pierced cling film and microwave on HIGH for 3½ minutes. Stir, cover and microwave on HIGH for a further 3½ minutes.
2. Drain off and discard most of the juice.
3. Whisk the egg whites until stiff. Whisk in the cream of tartar. Add 25g/1oz sugar and whisk until stiff again. Fold in the remaining sugar.
4. Pile on top of the fruit and microwave, uncovered, on HIGH for 2 minutes or until firm on top.

APRICOT BREAD PUDDING

Serves 2/215 calories per portion

75g/3oz wholemeal bread, sliced
25g/1oz ready-to-eat dried apricots, chopped
15ml/1 level tablespoon sultanas
10ml/2 level teaspoons honey
1 egg, size 3
150ml/¼ pint skimmed milk
Little grated lemon rind
Pinch dried mixed spice

1. Cut each slice of bread into 4 pieces. Place half in a dish. Top with apricots, sultanas and half of the honey. Cover with remaining bread and honey.
2. Beat egg with milk, lemon rind and spice. Pour over the bread.
3. Microwave on HIGH for 2½ minutes or until lightly set. Brown under the grill if desired.

MANGO SORBET

Serves 4/90 calories per portion

1 large mango, 375g/13oz,
    peeled and stoned
50g/2oz caster sugar
75ml/3floz water
15ml/1 tablespoon fresh
    lime juice
1 egg white

1. Place the sugar and water in a bowl and microwave on HIGH for 1½ minutes. Stir until the sugar is dissolved. Leave to cool.
2. Purée the mango flesh in a blender or food processor with the lime juice. Mix with the syrup.
3. Place in a shallow container. Cover and freeze until just mushy.
4. Place in a food processor and process until smooth. Whisk the egg white and fold in. Return to the container, cover and freeze until firm.
5. To serve microwave on DEFROST for about 2 minutes to soften slightly.

QUEEN OF PUDDINGS

Serves 2/195 calories per portion

1 egg, size 3, separated
5ml/1 level teaspoon fruit
    sugar (fructose)
75ml/3floz skimmed milk
2 drops vanilla essence
25g/1oz fresh white
    breadcrumbs
30ml/2 level tablespoons
    jam
25g/1oz caster sugar

1. Mix the egg yolk with the fruit sugar, skimmed milk and vanilla. Microwave on HIGH for 30 seconds.
2. Stir in the breadcrumbs and place in a serving dish. Microwave on HIGH for 30 seconds.
3. Spread jam on top.
4. Whisk egg white until stiff. Add the sugar and whisk until stiff again. Spread on top of the jam. Microwave on HIGH for 1½-2 minutes. Serve hot.

MANGO AND KIWI FRUIT TRIFLE

Serves 4/215 calories per portion

4 kiwi fruits, peeled
1 medium-sized ripe
mango, peeled, stoned and
cubed
4 sponge fingers
15ml/1 tablespoon Kirsch
or Cointreau or other
orange liqueur
15ml/1 tablespoon orange
juice
15g/½ oz plain flour
30ml/2 level tablespoons
cornflour
275ml/½ pint semi-
skimmed milk
25g/1oz caster sugar or
vanilla sugar
2 egg yolks
1 egg white
Few drops vanilla essence
if caster sugar is used

1. Cut 3 kiwi fruits into small cubes and divide between 4 sundae glasses with the mango.
2. Cut the sponge fingers into small pieces and place on top of the fruit.
3. Mix together the liqueur and orange juice and sprinkle on top.
4. In a large bowl mix the plain flour and cornflour with a little milk to make a smooth paste. Add the remaining milk and half the sugar. Whisk well to mix.
5. Microwave on HIGH until thick, whisking every ¾-1 minute. This should take about 4-5 minutes.
6. Lightly beat the egg yolks in a bowl with the vanilla if used. Gradually add 75ml/5 tablespoons hot custard, whisking well after every 15ml/1 tablespoon.
7. Whisk in the remaining custard. Microwave on HIGH for 3 seconds. Whisk well, then microwave for a further 30 seconds. Whisk well.
8. Cover with damp greaseproof paper and leave to cool.
9. Whisk the egg white until stiff. Add the remaining sugar and whisk until stiff again. Fold into the cooked custard.
10. Spoon custard on top of the fruit and sponge. Slice the remaining kiwi fruit and arrange on top.

STACKS OF SNACKS

Stock up your freezer with some of these low calorie snacks. Eat them on their own between meals or whenever you feel that your willpower is wavering. Or follow the serving suggestions to turn them into a complete light meal. You'll find soups, tasty spreads, burgers and lots more. Recipes make at least eight portions and can be reheated from frozen either conventionally or in a microwave.

DEVILLED CHICKEN

Serves 8/225 calories per portion

8 × 225g/8oz chicken leg joints, skin removed
15ml/1 level tablespoon tomato ketchup
15ml/1 level tablespoon Meaux mustard
10ml/2 teaspoons Worcestershire sauce
50g/2oz peach chutney
30ml/2 level tablespoons fresh brown breadcrumbs
Salt and pepper

1. Make 3 deep slits in the flesh of each chicken joint.
2. Mix remaining ingredients together.
3. Place a little of the devilled mixture into each slit.

To Freeze:
If cooking in a conventional oven, wrap chicken in foil, label and freeze. If using a microwave to cook the chicken at a later stage, wrap in cling film, then foil, label and freeze.

To Serve:
CONVENTIONAL: Defrost in refrigerator overnight. Cook at 180°C/350°F, gas mark 4, for 45 minutes to 1 hour until chicken is tender and juices run clear when pierced with a skewer.

MICROWAVE: Defrost for 5 minutes. Microwave on HIGH for 5 minutes.

Serving Suggestion:
Serve with a crisp green salad.

TUNA BURGERS

Makes 8/135 calories each

400g/14oz potato, peeled weight
10ml/2 level teaspoons low-fat spread
115g/4oz broccoli
115g/4oz mushrooms, chopped
198g/7oz can tuna in brine, drained, flaked
10ml/2 level teaspoons mixed dried herbs
Salt and freshly ground black pepper
2 eggs, size 3
175g/6oz fresh wholemeal breadcrumbs

1. Boil the potatoes; drain and mash with low-fat spread.
2. Boil broccoli for 3 minutes and drain, cool slightly and roughly chop.
3. Combine vegetables and tuna with the potato. Add the herbs and season to taste with salt and pepper.
4. Divide the mixture into 8 portions, form into burgers.
5. Lightly beat egg; dip the burgers into the egg, then coat with breadcrumbs.

To Freeze:
Open freeze. Wrap in freezer bags or film. Label and freeze.

To Serve:
CONVENTIONAL: Bake at 200°C/400°F, gas mark 6 for 25-30 minutes or until golden brown.

MICROWAVE: Not suitable.

Serving Suggestion:
Serve one tuna burger in a bap with shredded lettuce. The total cost will be 270 calories.

CORNED BEEF BURGERS

Serves 16/130 calories each

3 × 198g/7oz cans corned
beef, chopped
450g/1lb boiled potatoes,
mashed
8 pickled onions, chopped
15ml/1 tablespoon
chopped fresh parsley or
5ml/1 teaspoon dried
parsley
2 × 198g/7oz cans
sweetcorn, drained
1 egg, size 3, beaten
10ml/2 level teaspoons
mustard
Salt and pepper

1. Mash all the ingredients together using a fork, until well mixed.
2. Divide the mixture into 16 and shape into burgers.

To Freeze:
Open freeze. Wrap in freezer bags or freezer film, label and freeze.

To Serve:
CONVENTIONAL: Place under a moderate grill and cook for about 7 minutes on each side until browned and heated through.

MICROWAVE: Not suitable.

Serving Suggestion:
Serve one burger on toast or two with boiled vegetables.

RED KIDNEY BEAN BURGERS

Makes 16/155 calories each

450g/1lb brown rice
2 × 432g/15.2oz cans red
kidney beans, drained
175g/6oz onion, finely
chopped
4 cloves garlic, crushed
20ml/4 teaspoons soy
sauce
10ml/2 level teaspoons
ground ginger
10ml/2 level teaspoons
wholegrain mustard
20ml/4 teaspoons oil
Juice of 1 lemon
90ml/6 level tablespoons
tomato purée
Salt and black pepper

1. Cook rice in 1.15 litres/2 pints boiling water for 20 minutes.
2. Rinse beans, then cut in half.
3. Combine onion and garlic with the remaining seasonings.
4. Drain rice and add to mixture with beans. Mix thoroughly. Divide mixture into 16 and shape into burgers.

To Freeze:
Open freeze. Wrap in freezer bags or freezer film. Label and freeze.

To Serve:
CONVENTIONAL: Preheat oven to 180°C/350°F, gas mark 4. Bake burgers for 20-30 minutes until heated through.

MICROWAVE: Not suitable.

Serving Suggestion:
Serve two burgers with a crisp green salad.

PASTA AND BEAN SOUP (See picture opposite page 112)

Serves 8/150 calories per portion

225g/8oz canned pimentos, drained and chopped
225g/8oz carrots, peeled weight, chopped
350g/12oz onion, chopped
4 x 397g/14oz cans chopped tomatoes
4 chicken or vegetable stock cubes
4 bouquet garni
1.7l/3 pints water
115g/4oz small pasta shapes
350g/12oz canned cannellini beans, drained

1. Place pimentos, carrots and onion in a pan with the tomatoes, stock cubes, bouquet garni and water. Cover and simmer for 25 minutes.
2. Discard the bouquet garni, purée the soup in a blender or food processor.
3. Return to pan and bring to the boil.
4. Add the pasta and beans, cover and simmer for a further 10-15 minutes.
5. Divide the soup between eight containers.

To Freeze:
Leave to cool at the end of stage 5, wrap, label and freeze.

To Serve:
CONVENTIONAL: Thaw at room temperature overnight and place in a saucepan; reheat gently, stirring frequently, or reheat from frozen in a small pan over a low heat, stirring frequently.

MICROWAVE: Place one portion in a bowl and DEFROST for 13 minutes. Microwave on HIGH for 3 minutes or until hot, stirring once.

Serving Suggestion:
This is a filling soup served on its own or accompanied by a couple of crispbreads spread with skimmed milk soft cheese.

CURRIED BUTTER BEAN AND APPLE PÂTÉ
(See picture opposite page 81)

Serves 8/80 calories per portion

4 spring onions, leaves discarded, chopped
2 x 439g/15.5oz cans butter beans, drained
128g/4.5oz can apple purée
15ml/1 level tablespoon curry powder
60ml/4 level tablespoons low-fat natural yogurt
Black pepper

1. Place beans in a blender with apple purée, curry powder and yogurt. Season with black pepper. Blend until smooth.
2. Stir spring onions into the pâté.
3. Divide pâté between eight small containers.

To Freeze:
Cover with freezer film. Label and freeze.

To Serve:
Allow to thaw overnight in the refrigerator or for 3 hours at room temperature.

Serving Suggestion:
Accompany with a poppadum — some you can crisp in seconds in a microwave — for an extra cost of 65-75 calories.

LENTIL AND VEGETABLE SOUP (See picture opposite page 112)

Serves 8/150 carlories per portion

350g/12oz onion, diced
350g/12oz carrots, peeled
weight, diced
350g/12oz turnips, peeled
weight, diced
225g/8oz celery, diced
275g/10oz potato, peeled
weight, diced
175g/6oz split red lentils,
rinsed
4 chicken or vegetable
stock cubes
120ml/8 level tablespoons
tomato purée
4 bouquet garni
2.8 litres/5 pints water
Salt and pepper

1. Place vegetables in a saucepan with lentils.
2. Add stock cubes, tomato purée, bouquet garni and water. Season to taste.
3. Cover and simmer for 30 minutes.
4. Discard bouquet garni, purée half the soup in a blender or food processor, then mix with remaining soup.
5. Divide the soup between eight containers.

To Freeze:
Leave to cool at the end of stage 5, wrap, label and freeze.

To Serve:
CONVENTIONAL: Thaw at room temperature overnight and place in a saucepan; reheat gently, stirring frequently, or reheat from frozen in a small pan over a low heat, stirring frequently.

MICROWAVE: Place one portion in a bowl and DEFROST for 13 minutes. Microwave on HIGH for 3 minutes or until hot, stirring once.

Serving Suggestion:
Keep portions of this soup handy in your freezer to reheat quickly as a snack. Costs about the same as a bag of crisps and is much more nourishing and filling.

BAKED BEAN AND MUSHROOM PIZZA

Serves 8/120 calories per portion

2 × 225g/7.9oz can baked
beans in tomato sauce
115g/4oz mushrooms,
finely sliced
1 small onion, very finely
chopped
4 baps, 40g/1½oz each
75g/3oz Edam cheese,
grated

1. Mix the baked beans, mushrooms and onion together.
2. Split the baps in half.
3. Divide the baked bean mixture between the 8 halves.
4. Sprinkle with the cheese.

To Freeze:
Open freeze. Wrap each bap half in freezer film or put in a freezer bag. Label and freeze.

To Serve:
CONVENTIONAL: Place each bap under a moderate grill for 4-5 minutes until heated through and cheese is golden brown.

MICROWAVE: Not suitable.

CHICKEN AND SWEETCORN SOUP (See picture opposite page 112)

Serves 8/150 calories per portion

2 chicken breast portions,
175g/6oz each, skin
removed
350g/12oz carrots, peeled
weight, sliced
350g/12oz potatoes,
peeled weight, sliced
450g/1lb leeks, trimmed
weight, sliced
4 chicken stock cubes
2.8 litres/5 pints water
10ml/2 level teaspoons
dried thyme
Salt and pepper
350g/12oz canned or
frozen sweetcorn

1. Place chicken, carrots, potatoes and leeks in a saucepan.
2. Add the stock cubes, water and thyme. Season to taste with salt and pepper, cover and simmer for 30 minutes.
3. Remove chicken breast; discard the bones and chop the flesh.
4. Purée soup in a blender or food processor.
5. Return to pan with the chicken and sweetcorn. Cover and simmer for a further 5 minutes.
6. Divide the soup between eight containers.

To Freeze:
Leave to cool at the end of stage 6, wrap, label and freeze.

To Serve:
CONVENTIONAL: Thaw at room temperature overnight and place in a saucepan; reheat gently, stirring frequently, or reheat from frozen in a small pan over a low heat, stirring frequently.

MICROWAVE: Place one portion in a bowl and DEFROST for 13 minutes. Microwave on HIGH for 3 minutes or until hot, stirring once.

Serving Suggestion:
Toast a 25g/1oz slice of wholemeal bread and cut into squares. Sprinkle on top of soup before serving — costs an extra 60 calories.

SMOKED TROUT PÂTÉ

Serves 8/65 calories per portion

75g/3oz pickled dill
cucumbers, drained and
chopped
200g/7oz smoked trout
fillet, skin and bones
removed, flaked
275g/10oz tofu, crumbled
30ml/2 tablespoons cider
vinegar
5ml/1 level teaspoon
French mustard

1. Place trout in a blender with tofu, vinegar and mustard. Blend until smooth. Stir in chopped dill pickles.
2. Divide pâté between eight small containers.

To Freeze:
Cover with freezer film. Label and freeze.

To Serve:
CONVENTIONAL: Allow to thaw overnight in the refrigerator or for 3 hours at room temperature.

Serving Suggestion:
Spread on crispbreads and serve with carrot and celery sticks.

HAM AND CORN HASH CAKES (See picture opposite page 113)

Makes 8/140 calories per cake

275g/10oz potatoes, peeled
weight
15g/½oz low-fat spread
15ml/1 tablespoon
skimmed milk
115g/4oz self-raising flour
1 egg, size 3
75g/3oz cooked gammon,
lean only
75g/3oz canned
sweetcorn, drained
5ml/1 level teaspoon
mixed herbs
20ml/4 teaspoons oil

1. Boil potatoes until tender.
2. Drain and mash with low-fat spread and milk.
3. Stir flour into the potato and add beaten egg.
4. Mince or finely chop gammon and add to potatoes with sweetcorn and herbs. Make into 8 cakes.

To Freeze:
Open freeze, wrap in freezer bags or freezer film, label and freeze.

To Serve:
CONVENTIONAL: Heat 2.5ml/½ teaspoon oil in a non-stick pan for each cake. Turn cakes once during cooking so they are browned on both sides and heated right through.

MICROWAVE: Not suitable.

Serving Suggestion:
One or two cakes could be served with a crisp salad.

CORNED BEEF AND HORSERADISH SPREAD
(See picture opposite page 81)

Serves 8/85 calories per portion

½ green pepper,
deseeded, chopped
4 pickled onions, chopped
198g/7oz can corned beef,
cubed
200g/7oz skimmed milk
soft cheese
5ml/1 level teaspoon
horseradish sauce
60ml/4 tablespoons
skimmed milk

1. Place the corned beef in a blender with the cheese, horseradish sauce and skimmed milk. Blend until smooth.
2. Stir in chopped vegetables.
3. Divide spread between eight small containers.

To Freeze:
Cover with freezer film. Label and freeze.

To Serve:
Allow to thaw overnight in the refrigerator or for 3 hours at room temperature.

Serving Suggestion:
Use to make sandwiches. One portion will make two sandwiches using small 25g/1oz slices.

BLUE CHEESE AND WALNUT SPREAD
(See picture opposite page 81)

Serves 8/85 calories per portion

25g/1oz walnuts, chopped
75g/3oz Danish Blue cheese, crumbled
275g/10oz very-low-fat cottage cheese
45ml/3 tablespoons skimmed milk

1. Place the blue cheese in a blender or food processor with cottage cheese and skimmed milk. Blend until smooth.
2. Stir in the walnuts.
3. Divide spread between eight small containers.

To Freeze:
Cover with freezer film. Label and freeze.

To Serve:
Allow to thaw overnight in the refrigerator or for 3 hours at room temperature.

SKIPPERS PÂTÉ (See picture opposite page 81)

Serves 8/110 calories per portion

1 small onion, chopped
3 × 106g cans skippers in tomato sauce
115g/4oz fresh wholemeal breadcrumbs
30ml/2 tablespoons wine vinegar
45ml/3 level tablespoons tomato and chilli chutney
15ml/1 level tablespoon chopped parsley

1. Place the skippers and tomato sauce in a blender with breadcrumbs, vinegar, chutney and chopped parsley. Blend until smooth.
2. Stir in the onion.
3. Divide pâté between eight small containers.

To Freeze:
Cover with freezer film. Label and freeze.

To Serve:
Allow to thaw overnight in the refrigerator or for 3 hours at room temperature.

Serving Suggestion:
Pile on top of pumpernickle slices — 60 calories per 28g/1oz.

TUNA AND CHEESE TOASTS

Serves 8/215 calories per portion

2 × 198g/7oz cans tuna in brine
175g/6oz Edam cheese, grated
60ml/4 level tablespoons tomato ketchup
8 × 40g/1½oz slices wholemeal bread

1. Drain tuna and mix with the cheese and tomato ketchup.
2. Toast the bread.
3. Divide the tuna mixture into 8 and spread onto the 8 slices of toasted bread.

To Freeze:
Open freeze. Wrap each bread slice individually in freezer film. Label and freeze.

To Serve:
CONVENTIONAL: Grill tuna side up under a moderate heat for 4-5 minutes.

PEA AND HAM SOUP (See picture opposite page 112)

Serves 8/150 calories per portion

225g/8oz potato, peeled
weight, sliced
225g/8oz leeks, trimmed
weight, sliced
175g/6oz celery, sliced
10ml/2 level teaspoons
dried mint
1.71 litres/3 pints water
Salt and pepper
1.15kg/2½lb frozen peas
50g/2oz powdered
skimmed milk
115g/4oz lean cooked ham

1. Place the potato, leeks and celery in a pan with the mint and water. Season to taste with salt and pepper.
2. Cover and simmer for 10 minutes.
3. Add the peas and simmer for a further 10 minutes.
4. Purée the soup in a blender or food processor.
5. Add the milk powder and blend until evenly mixed.
6. Chop the ham and stir in.
7. Divide the soup between eight containers.

To Freeze:
Leave to cool at the end of stage 7, wrap, label and freeze.

To Serve:
CONVENTIONAL: Thaw at room temperature overnight and place in a saucepan; reheat gently, stirring frequently, or reheat from frozen in a small pan over a low heat, stirring frequently.

MICROWAVE: Place one portion in a bowl and DEFROST for 13 minutes. Microwave on HIGH for 3 minutes or until hot, stirring once.

Serving Suggestion:
Serve with a 50g/2oz piece of crusty French bread for a filling lunch costing 320 calories.

BACON AND BAKED BEAN SANDWICHES

Serves 8/170 calories per portion

115g/4oz streaky bacon,
rind removed
225g/7.9oz can baked
beans in tomato sauce
16 × 25g/1oz slices
wholemeal bread

1. Grill bacon well and roughly chop.
2. Mix bacon and beans together.
3. Make into eight sandwiches using the bread.

To Freeze:
Wrap each sandwich in freezer film or foil. Label and freeze.

To Serve:
CONVENTIONAL: Grill on both sides under a moderate grill until golden brown and heated through.

MICROWAVE: Not suitable.

BUTTER BEAN AND TOMATO STUFFING
(See picture opposite page 80)

Makes 12 portions/100 calories each

30ml/2 tablespoons oil
2 medium onions, chopped
3 cloves garlic, crushed
115g/4oz mushrooms, chopped
397g/14oz can chopped tomatoes
3 × 213g/7.5oz cans butter beans
250g/9oz wholemeal breadcrumbs
15ml/1 level tablespoon dried mixed herbs
45ml/3 level tablespoons chopped parsley

1. Heat oil in a non-stick pan and sauté onions and garlic for 2 minutes.
2. Mix together the onion, mushrooms, tomatoes, drained butter beans and breadcrumbs.
3. Add the herbs and parsley. Mix well.
4. Divide stuffing into twelve portions.

To Freeze:
Cover with freezer film. Label and freeze.

To Serve:
Allow to defrost then use to fill vegetables as follows...

STUFFED ONION

Serves 1/140 calories

1 large onion, 175g/6oz
1 portion Butter Bean and Tomato Stuffing (above)

Peel onion. Cut a large slice off base. Using a grapefruit knife cut out centre. Chop centre flesh and mix with stuffing. Place onion on a piece of foil and spoon stuffing into case. Fold foil into a parcel, place on baking tray and bake at 180°C/350°F, gas mark 4, for 45 minutes.

STUFFED PEPPER

Serves 1/140 calories (orange); 115 calories (red/green)

1 medium red, green or orange pepper, 150g/5oz
1 portion Butter Bean and Tomato Stuffing (above)

Slice off top of the pepper. Discard pith and seeds. Fill pepper with stuffing, then place in an ovenproof dish. Add 45ml/3 tablespoons water and replace the top. Bake at 190°C/375°F, gas mark 5, for 30 minutes.

STUFFED COURGETTES

Serves 1/140 calories

2 large courgettes, weighing 150g/5oz each
1 portion Butter Bean and Tomato Stuffing (above)

Blanch whole courgettes for 5 minutes. Drain and cool. Cut a slice off the side of each courgette and scoop out flesh. Chop flesh and mix with stuffing. Place courgette cases in an ovenproof dish and fill with stuffing. Add 15ml/1 tablespoon of water to the dish, then bake at 190°C/375°F, gas mark 5, for 25 minutes.

STUFFED SQUASH

Serves 1/195 calories

½ medium acorn squash, 275g/10oz (with skin)
1 portion Butter Bean and Tomato Stuffing (above)

Scoop out and discard seeds from squash. Place squash cut side down on a non-stick baking tray and bake at 190°C/375°F, gas mark 5, for 30 minutes. Turn squash over and spoon in filling. Return to the oven and bake for a further 20 minutes.

RICE AND BACON STUFFING

Makes 12 portions/100 calories each

150g/5oz brown rice
175g/6oz rashers streaky bacon
1 red pepper, deseeded and chopped
1 green pepper, deseeded and chopped
225g/8oz canned sweetcorn
225g/8oz frozen peas
40g/1½oz raisins

1. Boil rice, rinse in cold water and drain.
2. Well-grill the bacon, and chop it.
3. Mix rice and bacon with the peppers, sweetcorn and raisins. Add frozen peas (do not let peas defrost).
4. Divide stuffing into twelve portions.

To Freeze:
Cover with freezer film. Label and freeze.

To Serve:
Allow to defrost, then use to fill vegetables as follows. . .

STUFFED MUSHROOM

Serves 1/110 calories

1 large flat mushroom, 75g/3oz **1 portion stuffing**	Cut stem from mushroom and chop. Mix well with stuffing. Place mushroom in an ovenproof dish and spoon on stuffing. Pour water into the dish to come halfway up the sides of the mushroom, but not so that it touches the stuffing. Bake at 190°C/375°F, gas mark 5, for 30 minutes.

STUFFED MARROW

Serves 1/140 calories

½ small marrow, approx. 225g/8oz **1 portion stuffing**	Scoop out and discard seeds from marrow. Fill centre with stuffing. Place in an ovenproof dish, cover and cook at 180°C/350°F, gas mark 4, for 35 minutes.

STUFFED AUBERGINE

Serves 1/130 calories

1 medium aubergine, 200g/7oz **1 portion stuffing**	Blanch whole aubergine in boiling water for 8 minutes; drain and cool. Cut a slice off the side and scoop out flesh. Chop flesh and mix with stuffing. Place aubergine case in an ovenproof dish, fill with stuffing. Bake at 200°C/400°F, gas mark 6, for 25 minutes.

FREEZE YOURSELF SLIM MAIN MEALS

It will get your diet off to a good start if you prepare some of these low calorie meals in advance and freeze them ready to use. Each recipe can be divided into eight portions, so four recipes would give you a choice of main meals for a whole month. When you keep a stock of dieting meals in the freezer you can cut down on daily food shopping — and that means cutting down on being faced by all sorts of temptations. And if you do several recipes in one big cook-in, it means that you have to spend far less time each day preparing meals in the kitchen (a danger snacking area for many a dieter).

CHICKEN AND MUSHROOM COTTAGE PIE

Serves 8/385 calories per portion

1.8kg/4lbs potatoes,
peeled weight
2 medium onions, finely
chopped
450g/1lb mushrooms,
sliced
15ml/1 tablespoon oil
1.15 litres/2 pints hot
water
2 chicken stock cubes
50g/2oz cornflour
675g/1½lbs cooked
chicken, no skin, cubed
425g/15oz can chopped
tomatoes
5ml/1 level teaspoon dried
mixed herbs
Salt and pepper
2 eggs, size 3

1. Boil potatoes until tender.
2. Fry onions and mushrooms in oil until soft. Dissolve stock cubes in hot water.
3. Blend cornflour with a little cold water. Pour into a large saucepan with the stock. Bring to the boil, stirring continuously, then simmer for 1-2 minutes.
4. Add chicken, onions, mushrooms, tomatoes, herbs, salt, pepper to saucepan. Mix well.
5. Divide mixture between 8 ovenproof freezer containers.
6. Drain potatoes. Add eggs to potato and beat in well. Season. Pipe potato, using a star nozzle or spoon over chicken mixture.

To Freeze:
Cool quickly, seal, label and freeze.

To Serve:
CONVENTIONAL: Defrost in refrigerator overnight. Reheat at 200°C/400°F, gas mark 6 for 30 minutes or until heated through.
To reheat from frozen: preheat oven to 200°C/400°F, gas mark 6 and cook dish uncovered for 1¼ hours or until heated through.

MICROWAVE: Microwave on DEFROST for 8 minutes. Microwave on HIGH for 4-5 minutes.

Serving Suggestion:
Serve alone or accompanied with a green vegetable.

CHICKEN AND TARRAGON

Serves 8/235 calories per portion

275ml/½ pint water
1 chicken stock cube
25g/1oz cornflour
25g/1oz plain flour
8 skinless chicken breast fillets, 150g/5oz each
10ml/2 level teaspoons dried tarragon
425ml/¾ pint skimmed milk
25g/1oz low-fat spread
5ml/1 level teaspoon meaux mustard

1. Dissolve stock cube in the water. Place in a covered saucepan with chicken and 5ml/1 teaspoon of tarragon. Cook for 25-30 minutes, or until tender.
2. Drain stock and reserve. Place chicken fillets in 8 individual freezer containers.
3. Blend cornflour and plain flour with a little cold water until smooth.
4. Place in a saucepan with milk, low-fat spread, stock, mustard and remaining tarragon.
5. Bring to the boil, whisking continuously. Simmer for 1-2 minutes.
6. Pour sauce equally over each chicken fillet.

To Freeze:
Allow to cool. Seal, label and freeze in 8 individual freezer containers.

To Serve:
CONVENTIONAL: Defrost overnight in the refrigerator. Reheat gently in a saucepan until heated through.
To reheat from frozen: preheat oven to 190°C/375°F, gas mark 5, and reheat in a covered dish for 45 minutes-1 hour until heated through.

MICROWAVE: Microwave on DEFROST for 6 minutes. Microwave on HIGH for 2 minutes.

Serving Suggestion:
Green salad and a baked potato.

CANNELLONI WITH CHICKEN AND MUSHROOMS

Serves 8/330 calories per portion

16 tubes cannelloni,
225g/8oz
350g/12oz roast chicken,
skin removed
450g/1lb mushrooms,
sliced
5ml/1 level teaspoon
Marmite
40g/1½oz cornflour
40g/1½oz plain flour
1.15 litres/2 pints skimmed
milk
40g/1½oz low-fat spread
Salt and pepper
75g/3oz mature Cheddar
cheese, grated

1. Boil cannelloni in a large saucepan of water until just tender. Drain, rinse under cold water and lay on kitchen paper.
2. Cut the roast chicken into small pieces.
3. Place the sliced mushrooms, Marmite and 275ml/½ pint water in a saucepan and simmer for 5 minutes uncovered. Drain.
4. Blend the cornflour and plain flour with a little skimmed milk until smooth. Place in a saucepan with the remaining milk and low-fat spread.
5. Bring to the boil, whisking, and simmer for 1-2 minutes. Season.
6. Mix chicken and mushrooms together with 275ml/½ pint sauce. Season to taste.
7. Spoon mixture into cannelloni tubes, dividing it equally.
8. Place 2 tubes in each of 8 ovenproof freezer containers.
9. Pour remaining sauce over cannelloni and sprinkle cheese on top.

To Freeze:
Allow to cool. Cover, label and freeze.

To Serve:
CONVENTIONAL: Remove lid and reheat at 200°C/400°F, gas mark 6, for 50-55 minutes.

MICROWAVE: Microwave on DEFROST for 5 minutes. Microwave on HIGH for 1½ minutes or until hot.

Serving Suggestion:
A crisp green salad.

SWEET AND SOUR CHICKEN

Serves 8/225 calories per portion

8 × 175g/6oz chicken breasts
15ml/1 tablespoon oil
1 green pepper, deseeded and cut into strips
1 red pepper, deseeded and cut into strips
6 spring onions, leaves discarded, sliced
45ml/3 tablespoons Soy sauce
45ml/3 tablespoons white wine vinegar
5ml/1 level teaspoon ground ginger
227g/8oz can pineapple pieces in natural juice
225ml/8floz water
60ml/4 level tablespoons cornflour
2 medium oranges, peeled and pith discarded

1. Grill chicken breasts until cooked through and remove skin. Place in 8 individual freezer dishes.
2. Heat oil in a saucepan and gently fry the peppers and spring onions for 3-4 minutes.
3. Add Soy sauce, white wine vinegar and ginger. Stir-fry for 1 minute.
4. Drain pineapple reserving 120ml/8 tablespoons of juice and add remaining juice to pan.
5. Blend cornflour with remaining pineapple juice and stir into the saucepan with the water. Bring to the boil, stir continuously and simmer for 2 minutes.
6. Stir in pineapple pieces and orange segments. Stir into sauce.

To Freeze:
Spoon sauce over chicken portions. Allow to cool, seal, label and freeze.

To Serve:
CONVENTIONAL: Defrost overnight in the refrigerator and reheat uncovered in a saucepan over a low heat. Or cook from frozen at 190°C/375°F, gas mark 5, for 1½ hours or until heated through.

MICROWAVE: Microwave on DEFROST for 7 minutes. Microwave on HIGH for 3 minutes or until hot.

Serving Suggestion:
Serve with boiled rice.

TURKEY AND CRANBERRY CASSEROLE

Serves 8/345 calories per portion

8 × 225g/8oz turkey breast
fillets
16 button onions or 2
large
4 sticks celery
225g/8oz button
mushrooms
225g/8oz cranberry sauce
575ml/1 pint water
1½ chicken stock cubes
60ml/4 level tablespoons
cornflour
Salt and pepper

1. Place all the ingredients except the cornflour into a large casserole dish.
2. Cook at 180°C/350°F, gas mark 4, for 2 hours.
3. Blend cornflour with a little cold water until smooth and stir into the casserole. Cover and cook for a further 15 minutes.

To Freeze:
Divide between 8 individual freezer containers. Seal, label and freeze.

To Serve:
CONVENTIONAL: Reheat in a covered casserole dish at 190°C/375°F, gas mark 5, for 1¼ hours. Or defrost overnight in the refrigerator and reheat, covered, at 200°C/400°F, gas mark 6, for 30-40 minutes until hot. Stir occasionally.

MICROWAVE: Microwave on DEFROST for 9 minutes. Microwave on HIGH for 4 minutes.

Serving Suggestion:
Serve with Duchesse or mashed potatoes and green vegetables.

CHICKEN AND CORN CASSEROLE

Serves 8/220 calories per portion

8 × 175g/6oz chicken
breasts
2 × 200g/7oz cans
sweetcorn, drained
2 medium onions, sliced
425g/15oz can tomatoes
575ml/1 pint water
1 chicken stock cube
Chicken seasoning
Salt and pepper
60ml/4 level tablespoons
cornflour

1. Grill chicken pieces for 5 minutes on each side. Remove skin and discard it.
2. Place sweetcorn, onions, tomatoes and their juice, water, stock cube and seasonings into a large saucepan.
3. Bring to the boil and simmer for 5 minutes.
4. Blend cornflour with a little cold water and stir into sauce.
5. Bring back to the boil and simmer for 2 minutes, stirring continuously.
6. Place chicken pieces in a large casserole dish and pour sauce over. Check seasoning.
7. Cover and cook at 180°C/350°F, gas mark 4, for 1 hour.

To Freeze:
Divide between 8 individual freezer containers; cool, seal, label and freeze.

To Serve:
CONVENTIONAL: Cook covered at 190°C/375°F, gas mark 5, for 1 hour 30 minutes. Or defrost overnight in the refrigerator and reheat at 200°C/400°F, gas mark 6, for 30-45 minutes.

MICROWAVE: Microwave on DEFROST for 9 minutes. Microwave on HIGH for 3 minutes, or until hot.

Serving Suggestion:
Serve with boiled potatoes and green beans.

MEATBALLS IN ST CLEMENTS SAUCE

Serves 8/290 calories per portion

1 medium onion, finely
chopped
800g/1¾ lbs extra lean
minced beef
115g/4oz fresh
breadcrumbs
Salt and pepper
2.5ml/½ level teaspoon
dried ground sage
2 eggs, size 3, beaten
1 medium onion, chopped
finely
30ml/2 level tablespoons
honey
15ml/1 level tablespoon
English mustard
10ml/2 teaspoons
Worcestershire sauce
Grated rind and juice of 2
oranges
45ml/3 tablespoons lemon
juice
30ml/2 level tablespoons
tomato ketchup
575ml/1 pint water
Salt and pepper
30ml/2 level tablespoons
cornflour

1. Mix onion, beef, breadcrumbs, salt and pepper, sage and eggs together.
2. Roll mixture between wetted palms of hands and make into 40 meatballs (about golf-ball size).
3. Arrange in a single layer in a large roasting tin or a shallow ovenproof dish.
4. Put onion, honey, mustard, Worcestershire sauce, orange juice and rind, lemon juice, tomato ketchup, water and seasoning in a saucepan. Bring to the boil, stirring. Check seasoning and pour over meatballs.
5. Cover dish loosely with foil and cook at 180°C/350°F, gas mark 4, for 1¼ hours.
6. Remove meatballs and divide between eight containers.
7. Blend the cornflour with a little extra cold water and stir into sauce. Pour into a pan and bring to the boil, simmer for 1-2 minutes.
8. Pour sauce over the meatballs.

To Freeze:
Leave to cool at end of stage 8, wrap, label and freeze.

To Serve:
CONVENTIONAL: Thaw at room temperature for 4-5 hours. Put into a saucepan and heat through gently or heat in an oven at 180°C/350°F, gas mark 4 for 30 minutes. Alternatively, reheat from frozen at 180°C/350°F, gas mark 4, for 1 hour.

MICROWAVE: Place one portion in a covered dish and microwave on DEFROST for 6 minutes. Cook on HIGH for 2½ minutes.

Serving Suggestion:
Good served with instant mashed potato or a jacket baked potato. Count 90 calories for each 28g/1oz dry weight instant mashed potato made up with water. A jacket baked potato (200g/7oz raw weight) costs 150 calories.

LAMB PARCELS

Serves 8/235 calories per portion

8 × 150g/5oz lamb leg steaks, trimmed of fat
Lamb seasoning
Dried mint
Salt and pepper
85g/3oz packet thyme and parsley stuffing mix
1 green pepper, deseeded and diced
2 medium onions, sliced
10ml/2 teaspoons oil
10ml/2 teaspoons Worcestershire sauce
8 tomatoes, skinned, seeds removed and chopped

1. Sprinkle both sides of lamb steaks with lamb seasoning, dried mint, salt and pepper.
2. Place each lamb steak on a piece of foil large enough to make up a loose parcel.
3. Make up stuffing mix as directed on the packet using boiling water only.
4. Put oil and Worcestershire sauce in a non-stick pan and fry onion and pepper for 5 minutes.
5. Stir onion and pepper mixture into stuffing mix.
6. Add the tomatoes to the stuffing mixture and mix well.
7. Divide the stuffing mixture between the 8 lamb steaks, placing it on top of each.
8. Fold foil loosely to make parcels and seal the edges.

To Freeze:
Place foil parcels in a polythene bag. Label and freeze.

To Serve:
CONVENTIONAL: Defrost overnight in refrigerator. Cook in foil at 180°C/350°F, gas mark 4, for 35-45 minutes until lamb steak is tender.

MICROWAVE: Remove from foil and place in a suitable dish. Microwave on DEFROST, covered, for 6 minutes. Using a browning dish, heat the dish for 6 minutes. Add lamb steak and microwave on HIGH for 3 minutes.

Serving Suggestion:
Serve garnished with watercress and serve with two vegetables of your choice.

BEEF CARBONNADE MARINADE (See picture opposite page 113)

Serves 2/220 calories per portion

**225g/8oz beef topside
2 cloves garlic
6 peppercorns
150ml/¼ pint Guinness
10ml/2 level teaspoons
brown sugar
10ml/2 level teaspoons
Dijon mustard
10ml/2 level teaspoons
tomato purée
Salt and pepper
175g/6oz mushrooms**

1. Discard any fat from beef then cut into bite-sized chunks.
2. Crush garlic, then put in a bowl with peppercorns, Guinness, sugar, mustard, tomato purée and salt and pepper. Mix together.
3. Add beef and mushrooms to the marinade and leave in a refrigerator for 2-4 hours.

To Freeze:
Put in a freezer container, label and freeze.

To Serve:
CONVENTIONAL: Defrost overnight in refrigerator for 00 hours at room temperature. Take the beef and mushrooms from the marinade, put on an ovenproof tray and grill on both sides for 5 minutes. Place the marinade in a saucepan, bring to the boil and simmer until reduced by half. Arrange meat and vegetables on a serving dish and pour over marinade.

MICROWAVE: Not suitable.

Serving Suggestion:
Cut 115g/4oz courgettes into slices and grill with meat and mushrooms, coated in a little of the marinade. Adds just 15 calories.

OLD ENGLISH RABBIT CASSEROLE

Serves 8/250 calories per portion

900g/2lb rabbit, boneless,
fresh or frozen, thawed
25g/1oz plain flour
30ml/2 tablespoons oil
2 medium onions, finely
chopped
175g/6oz mushrooms,
sliced
175g/6oz carrots, chopped
2 dessert apples
150ml/¼ pint red wine
275ml/10floz water
1 chicken stock cube
1 bouquet garni
50g/2oz raisins
Grated rind and juice of 1
orange
Salt and pepper

1. Rinse the rabbit and pat dry with kitchen paper. Cut into cubes.
2. Coat the rabbit in flour and fry in oil in a non-stick pan until browned.
3. Remove meat from frying pan and place in a large casserole dish, with the onions, mushrooms and carrots.
4. Peel and core the apples and roughly chop. Dissolve stock cube in water. Add to casserole with the raisins, rind and juice of orange, wine, bouquet garni and seasoning.
5. Cover and place in oven at 180°C/350°F, gas mark 4 for 1½ hours.

To Freeze:
Cool quickly and divide between 8 individual freezer containers, seal, label and freeze.

To Serve:
CONVENTIONAL: Thaw overnight in refrigerator and reheat in a saucepan over a low heat. Or place in oven from frozen at 190°C/375°F, gas mark 5 and reheat covered for 1 hour or until hot.

MICROWAVE: Place one portion in a suitable dish and microwave on DEFROST for 4 minutes. Microwave on HIGH for 2 minutes.

VENISON CASSEROLE

Serves 8/235 calories per portion

900g/2lb venison, cubed
275ml/½ pint dry red
wine
115g/4oz carrots, sliced
4 whole cloves
A few peppercorns
1 medium onion, chopped
15ml/1 tablespoon oil
450g/1lb button
mushrooms
225g/8oz button onions
575ml/1 pint water
1 beef stock cube
Salt and pepper
25g/1oz cornflour

1. Put venison in a bowl and add red wine, sliced carrots, cloves, peppercorns and onion. Marinade for 2 hours or overnight in refrigerator.
2. Drain the venison, reserving marinade and fry in a non-stick pan in the oil.
3. Place in a casserole dish with mushrooms, onions, marinade, water, stock cube and seasoning.
4. Cover and cook at 170°C/325°F, gas mark 3 for 2½ hours.
5. Blend cornflour with a little cold water and stir into the casserole. Return to the oven for a further 15 minutes.

To Freeze:
Cool quickly, divide between 8 individual freezer containers, seal, label and freeze.

To Serve:
CONVENTIONAL: Defrost overnight in the refrigerator and reheat in a saucepan over a low heat. Or, cook from frozen at 180°C/350°F, gas mark 4, for 1¼ hours until heated through.

MICROWAVE: Microwave on DEFROST for 6 minutes. Microwave on HIGH for 2 minutes.

FRICASSÉE OF VEAL

Serves 8/275 calories per portion

1.15kg/2½lbs stewing veal, fat and gristle removed and chopped into 4cm/1½ inch squares
450g/1lb baby carrots or larger carrots cut into finger-sized pieces
2 medium onions, chopped
5ml/1 level teaspoon dried thyme or 15ml/1 level tablespoon fresh thyme, chopped
1½ chicken stock cubes
850ml/1½ pints boiling water
150ml/¼ pint dry white wine
Salt and pepper
50g/2oz low-fat spread
50g/2oz plain flour
15ml/1 level tablespoon cornflour
50g/2oz skimmed milk powder

1. Place veal in a saucepan, cover with cold water, bring to the boil and simmer for 1 minute. Strain through a colander and rinse meat to remove all scum. Rinse out the pan thoroughly and replace the meat.
2. Put carrots, onion and thyme into the pan.
3. Dissolve the stock cubes in the water and add to the pan with the wine. Bring slowly to the boil. Season. Cover and simmer gently for about 1 hour.
4. Divide the veal and vegetables between eight individual containers.
5. Strain the stock into a measuring jug, make up to 1 litre/1¼ pints with water if necessary and return to the pan. Add the low-fat spread and heat gently. Blend the flour, cornflour and skimmed milk powder with a little water until smooth.
6. Whisk into the pan and simmer for 2 minutes, whisking continuously. Check seasoning. Pour over the meat and vegetables (strain if necessary).

To Freeze:
Leave to cool, wrap, label and freeze at the end of stage 6.

To Serve:
CONVENTIONAL: Thaw at room temperature for 3 hours or overnight in refrigerator. Reheat in a small saucepan, stirring frequently.

MICROWAVE: Put one portion in a suitable dish and microwave on DEFROST for 8 minutes, stirring every 2 minutes to move frozen pieces to outside. Microwave on HIGH for 3 minutes.

RABBIT IN MUSTARD SAUCE

Serves 8/220 calories per portion

900g/2lb rabbit, boneless, fresh or frozen (thawed)
25g/1oz plain flour
5ml/1 level teaspoon dry English mustard
30ml/2 tablespoons oil
2 medium onions, finely chopped
1 chicken or vegetable stock cube
425ml/¾ pint water
30ml/2 level tablespoons cornflour
25g/1oz skimmed milk powder
15ml/1 level tablespoon whole grain mustard
15ml/1 level tablespoon chives, chopped
15ml/1 level tablespoon parsley, chopped
Salt and pepper

1. Rinse the rabbit and pat dry with kitchen paper, then cut into cubes.
2. Mix flour and English mustard together and coat rabbit.
3. Heat oil in a non-stick pan and fry rabbit until brown. Place in a large saucepan.
4. Add onions, stock cube and water.
5. Cover and simmer for 1 hour.
6. Blend cornflour and skimmed milk powder together with a little cold water. Stir into saucepan, add whole grain mustard, chives, parsley, salt and pepper.
7. Simmer for 5 minutes, stirring all the time.

To Freeze:
Cool quickly and divide between 8 individual freezer containers. Seal, label and freeze.

To Serve:
CONVENTIONAL: Defrost overnight in the refrigerator and reheat in a saucepan over a low heat or cook from frozen at 190°C/375°F, gas mark 5, for 1¼ hours or until heated through.

MICROWAVE: Microwave on DEFROST for 4 minutes. Microwave on HIGH for 2 minutes.

Serving Suggestion:
Baked potato and green beans.

KIDNEYS IN SHERRY SAUCE

Serves 8/185 calories per portion

2 medium onions, finely chopped
15ml/1 tablespoon oil
900g/2lb lambs' kidneys
225g/8oz button mushrooms
40g/1½ oz plain flour
575ml/1 pint water
1 beef or lamb stock cube
200ml/7floz dry sherry
30ml/2 level tablespoons redcurrant jelly
Salt and pepper

1. Fry onions in the oil in a non-stick pan until golden brown.
2. Wash, skin and core the kidneys and cut each into 3 pieces.
3. Add kidneys and mushrooms to the onions and fry for 5 minutes, stirring continuously.
4. Add the flour, water, stock cube, sherry and redcurrant jelly. Season and bring to the boil and simmer for 15 minutes.

To Freeze:
Cool quickly and divide between 8 individual freezer containers. Seal, label and freeze.

To Serve:
CONVENTIONAL: Cook from frozen at 180°C/350°F, gas mark 4 for 30 minutes until heated through OR defrost overnight in the refrigerator and reheat in a small saucepan over a low heat.

MICROWAVE: Microwave on DEFROST for 4 minutes. Microwave on HIGH for 1 minute.

Serving Suggestion:
Served on a bed of boiled rice.

LIVER MEXICAN

Serves 8/260 calories per portion

900g/2lb lambs' liver, tubes discarded
2 medium onions, sliced
1 red pepper, deseeded and sliced
1 green pepper, deseeded and sliced
425g/15oz can chopped tomatoes
275g/10oz can red kidney beans, drained and rinsed
275ml/½ pint water
1 stock cube
Salt and pepper
25g/1oz cornflour

1. Rinse liver under cold water and pat dry with kitchen paper. Place in a casserole dish.
2. Sprinkle onions and peppers over the liver.
3. Pour can of chopped tomatoes over liver and stir in red kidney beans.
4. Dissolve stock cube in water, pour over liver, season to taste and mix well.
5. Cover and cook at 180°C/350°F, gas mark 4, for 1 hour.
6. Blend cornflour with a little cold water. Stir into casserole and return to the oven for a further 20 minutes.

To Freeze:
Cool quickly. Divide between 8 individual freezer containers. Seal, label and freeze.

To Serve:
CONVENTIONAL: Defrost overnight in refrigerator and reheat in a saucepan over a low heat. Or, cook from frozen at 190°C/375°F, gas mark 5, for 1 hour.

MICROWAVE: Microwave on DEFROST for 5 minutes. Microwave on HIGH for 2 minutes.

Serving Suggestion:
Baked potato and carrots, or served with boiled rice.

PORK CHOPS IN APRICOT SAUCE

Serves 8/300 calories per portion

8 x 185g/6½ oz pork chops, trimmed of fat
2 x 283g/10oz can apricots in natural juice
15ml/1 tablespoon Worcestershire sauce
25g/1oz soft brown sugar
15ml/1 tablespoon vinegar
15ml/1 tablespoon lemon juice
150ml/¼ pint water
30ml/2 level tablespoons cornflour

1. Grill chops well. Place each chop in a freezer container or small freezer bag.
2. Drain apricots and reserve juice. Roughly chop three-quarters of the apricots and put in a saucepan with 150ml/¼ pint reserved juice, Worcestershire sauce, brown sugar, vinegar and lemon juice.
3. Bring to the boil and simmer uncovered for 10 minutes.
4. Blend cornflour with a little cold water and pour into sauce with remaining water. Stirring continuously, bring back to the boil, then simmer for 2-3 minutes.
5. Divide sauce into eight portions and put in freezer container with the chops.

To Freeze:
Cool, seal, label and freeze.

To Serve:
CONVENTIONAL: Defrost in refrigerator overnight and reheat in a covered dish at 190°C/375°F, gas mark 5, for 45 minutes or until heated. Or cook from frozen at 180°C/350°F, gas mark 4, for 1¼ hours or until heated through.

MICROWAVE: Microwave on DEFROST for 8 minutes. Microwave on HIGH for 4 minutes.

Serving Suggestion:
Serve with boiled rice (brown 99 calories per 28g/1oz weighed dry; white 102 calories) and green beans (7 calories per 28g/1oz) or peas (19 calories per 28g/1oz fresh; 15 calories frozen).

PORK AND MUSHROOM CASSEROLE

Serves 8/220 calories per portion

1.15kg/2½lbs pork fillet or tenderloin, trimmed of fat, cut into bite-sized pieces
450g/1lb button mushrooms, halved
2 medium onions, finely chopped
10ml/2 level teaspoons dried mixed herbs
275ml/½ pint hot water
1 chicken or vegetable stock cube
28g/1oz cornflour
28g/1oz skimmed milk powder
Salt and pepper

1. Dissolve stock cube in water.
2. Place pork, mushrooms, onions, herbs and stock in a large casserole.
3. Cover and cook at 180°C/350°F, gas mark 4, for 1¾ hours or until pork is tender.
4. Blend cornflour and skimmed milk powder with a little cold water until smooth. Stir into casserole, season to taste and return to oven for a further 20 minutes.
5. Divide between 8 individual freezer containers.

To Freeze:
Allow to cool. Seal, label and freeze.

To Serve:
CONVENTIONAL: Defrost overnight in the refrigerator. Reheat in a saucepan over a low heat until heated through. To reheat from frozen: place in a preheated oven, 180°C/350°F, gas mark 4, and reheat covered for 1½ hours. Or, alternatively place in a saucepan over a low heat, and heat until hot, stirring occasionally.

MICROWAVE: Microwave on DEFROST for 2 minutes. Stir and defrost for a further 3 minutes. Microwave on HIGH for 2 minutes.

Serving Suggestion:
Serve with a baked potato and a green vegetable.

PRAWN AND COD PANCAKES

Serves 8/275 calories per portion

Batter
225g/8oz plain flour
Pinch salt
575ml/1 pint skimmed milk
2 eggs, size 3
5ml/1 teaspoon corn oil

Filling
227g/8oz can prawns
350g/12oz fresh cod fillet
¼ fish stock cube
150ml/¼ pint boiling water
275ml/½ pint skimmed milk
1 bay leaf
1 medium onion, chopped
5ml/1 level teaspoon dill weed
45ml/3 level tablespoons cornflour
15ml/1 level tablespoon Parmesan cheese
30ml/2 tablespoons lemon juice
Salt and pepper
115g/4oz low-fat Cheddar cheese, grated

1. Make a batter with the flour, salt, skimmed milk and eggs.
2. Brush a non-stick frying pan or omelet pan with a little of the oil and heat.
3. Pour in just enough batter to thinly coat the base and cook until the underneath is set. Toss or turn over and cook the other side. Slide pancake onto a plate.
4. Make another 15 pancakes in the same way. Stack them on a plate with a piece of greaseproof paper between each pancake.
5. Drain and rinse the prawns. Set aside.
6. Place fish in a saucepan. Dissolve the stock cube in the boiling water. Pour over the fish together with the skimmed milk. Add the bay leaf and bring to the boil. Simmer for 8-10 minutes until fish is just cooked.
7. Remove the fish from the pan and flake the flesh removing skin and any bones. Set aside.
8. Strain the cooking liquid into a measuring jug and make up to 425ml/¾ pint with water if necessary.
9. Put cooking liquid, onion and dill into a pan. Mix cornflour with a little cold water and add. Bring to the boil, stirring and simmer for 1-2 minutes until thickened.
10. Stir in the prawns, fish, Parmesan, lemon juice and seasoning.
11. Place equal amounts along the centre of each pancake, and roll up (or fold pancakes into quarters and fill 'pocket' with fish mixture).
12. Put 2 pancakes in each 8 small freezer containers.

To Freeze:
Leave to cool at end of stage 12, wrap, label and freeze.

To Serve:
CONVENTIONAL: Reheat from frozen covered loosely with foil for 20 minutes at 200°C/400°F, gas mark 6. Uncover and sprinkle with 15g/½oz low-fat Cheddar cheese and cook uncovered for a further 20-25 minutes.

MICROWAVE: Put two pancakes in a suitable dish and microwave on DEFROST for 7 minutes. Microwave on HIGH for 2 minutes.

Serving Suggestion:
Serve with a crisp green salad. A mix of lettuce, cucumber, pepper and cress won't cost more than 25 calories a serving.

FREEZER SOUPS
Pasta and Bean; Lentil and
Vegetable; Pea and Ham; Chicken
and Sweetcorn

FREEZER MEALS
Beef Carbonnade
Marinade; Ham and
Corn Hash Cakes

PORK, APPLE AND PRUNE MEATBALLS

Serves 8/345 calories per portion

Meatballs
675g/1½lbs lean ground or minced pork
75g/3oz fresh wholemeal breadcrumbs
2 medium eating apples, peeled, cored and grated
1 small onion, grated
2 eggs, size 3, lightly beaten
2.5ml/½ level teaspoon ground allspice
Salt and pepper
32 no-soak prunes
Sauce
2 large onions, thinly sliced
275ml/½ pint dry still cider
1 chicken stock cube
275ml/½ pint boiling water
150ml/¼ pint unsweetened apple juice
10 juniper berries, crushed
1 bay leaf
30ml/2 level tablespoons cornflour
Salt and pepper
120ml/8 tablespoons low-fat natural yogurt

1. Place all the meatball ingredients except prunes, in a bowl, mix well. With wetted hands take a small amount of meat mixture and flatten slightly. Place a prune in the centre and carefully draw the meat mixture up around the sides and top of the prune. Roll to form a ball. Repeat with remaining 31 prunes.
2. Place the onions, cider, water, crumbled stock cube, apple juice, juniper berries, bay leaf and cornflour into a pan. Bring to the boil, stirring, and simmer for 1-2 minutes. Season.
3. Arrange the meatballs in a single layer in a baking dish. Pour the sauce over the meatballs. Cover loosely with foil and bake at 200°C/400°F, gas mark 6 for 45-55 minutes, stirring occasionally, until cooked.

To Freeze:
Divide between 8 individual containers. Wrap, label and freeze.

To Serve:
CONVENTIONAL: Thaw overnight in refrigerator or 4 hours at room temperature. Place in a pan, cover and reheat for 15-20 minutes until thoroughly heated. Remove meatballs and stir 15ml/1 level tablespoon yogurt into sauce. Pour over meat.

MICROWAVE: Microwave on DEFROST for 8-10 minutes. Microwave on HIGH for 1 minute. Remove meat and stir 15ml/1 tablespoon yogurt into sauce. Pour sauce over meat.

STUFFED COD STEAKS

Serves 8/200 calories per portion

8 × 275g/10oz cod steaks, weighed with bone
10ml/2 level teaspoons low-fat spread
1 small onion, finely chopped
5ml/1 teaspoon oil
75g/3oz streaky bacon, back rasher
50g/2oz mushrooms, finely chopped
40g/1½oz fresh wholemeal breadcrumbs
Salt and pepper
150ml/¼ pint skimmed milk

1. Wash cod steaks and remove the central bone with a sharp pointed knife and place the fish in an ovenproof dish which has been greased with the low-fat spread.
2. Fry the onion in the oil until soft.
3. Well-grill the bacon rashers and when cool, chop finely.
4. Mix mushrooms with onions, bacon, breadcrumbs and salt and pepper. Bind together using a little of the milk.
5. Fill the centre of each steak with the stuffing, secure the 'flaps' of the fish with wooden cocktail sticks and place in casserole dish.
6. Pour remaining milk over the cod steaks.
7. Cover and bake at 170°C/325°F, gas mark 3 for 30 minutes or until fish is tender.

To Freeze:
Cool quickly, remove cocktail sticks and wrap individually in foil. Seal, label and freeze.

To Serve:
CONVENTIONAL: Place from frozen in preheated oven 180°C/350°F, gas mark 4 for 45 minutes or until heated through. Or, thaw overnight in refrigerator and reheat at 180°C/350°F, gas mark 4 for 20-30 minutes or until hot.

MICROWAVE: Microwave on DEFROST for 5 minutes. Microwave on HIGH for 2 minutes.

Serving Suggestion:
Delicious with new potatoes and green beans. Add a couple of tablespoons of low-calorie seafood sauce if you wish — 20 calories per 15ml/1 level tablespoon.

SMOKED HADDOCK AND BROCCOLI LAYER

Serves 8/230 calories per portion

675g/1½lbs smoked haddock
225g/8oz mushrooms, sliced
575ml/1 pint skimmed milk
900g/2lbs broccoli
20g/¾oz cornflour
20g/¾oz plain flour
20g/¾oz low-fat spread
8 tomatoes
115g/4oz mature Cheddar cheese, grated
Salt and pepper

1. Put the haddock, mushrooms and milk in a saucepan and cook uncovered for 15 minutes or until fish is tender and flakes easily.
2. Strain, reserving the milk, and flake the fish.
3. Cook the broccoli in boiling water for 8 minutes.
4. Blend the cornflour and plain flour with a little cold water to make a smooth paste.
5. Place in a saucepan with milk and low-fat spread. Bring to the boil, whisking and simmer for 1-2 minutes.
6. Add haddock and mushrooms to sauce, season to taste.
7. Skin and slice the tomatoes.
8. In 8 individual freezer containers, place a layer of broccoli, haddock and mushroom mixture and tomatoes.
9. Sprinkle each portion with 15g/½oz grated cheese.

To Freeze:
Cool quickly, cover, label and freeze.

To Serve:
CONVENTIONAL: Cook uncovered from frozen at 200°C/400°F, gas mark 6, for 1 hour or until heated through. Or thaw overnight in the refrigerator and reheat at 200°C/400°F, gas mark 6, for 30 minutes or until heated through.

MICROWAVE: Microwave on DEFROST for 8 minutes. Microwave on HIGH for 5 minutes.

Serving Suggestion:
Serve on its own or with sweetcorn.

VEGETABLE MIXES AND DISHES

Make good use of vegetables when you are dieting: they could be a big help in getting you to your target weight in the fastest possible time. Because most vegetables are low in calories this means that vegetarian meals are often bulkier than meat or fish meals of the same calories. And as vegetable meals tend to be high in fibre and low in saturated fat, you will be following good health guidelines when you select dishes from this chapter. You'll find here complete meals to freeze, vegetable mixes that you can use to accompany a main course and some recipes that you can serve up either way. If you are choosing entirely vegetarian meals when you are dieting, remember to include recipes that use peas, beans or lentils which are valuable sources of protein and select from as wide a variety of dishes as possible.

CHEESY RICE FILLED COURGETTES

Serves 8/105 calories

75g/3oz long-grain brown rice
225ml/8floz water
1.25ml/¼ level teaspoon salt
4 large courgettes (175-200g/6-7oz each), stalk removed and halved
75g/3oz cottage cheese
25g/1oz walnuts, chopped
50g/2oz canned sweetcorn
30ml/2 level tablespoons parsley, chopped
Pepper
50g/2oz reduced fat Cheddar cheese, grated

1. Put the rice in a pan with the water and salt. Cover the pan and bring to the boil. Stir well. Cover and simmer gently for 40 minutes until tender. Drain. Check occasionally and if necessary add a little extra water to prevent sticking.
2. Scoop out the flesh from the courgette shells using a teaspoon (freeze to use in soups or casseroles) leaving a shell 0.5cm/¼ inch thick.
3. Blanch the courgette shells in boiling, salted water for 3-4 minutes. Drain, plunge into ice-cold water. Drain and dry thoroughly.
4. Mix the rice, cottage cheese, walnuts, sweetcorn, parsley, salt and pepper.
5. Fill the courgette shells with the rice mixture.

To Freeze:
At the end of stage 5, wrap each courgette half individually, then label and freeze.

To Serve:
CONVENTIONAL: Thaw at room temperature for 4 hours or overnight in a refrigerator. Reheat at 190°C/375°F, gas mark 5, for 15 minutes, loosely covered. Uncover and sprinkle with 15g/½oz grated cheese and bake for a further 10 minutes. Alternatively, reheat from frozen at 200°C/400°F, gas mark 6, for 20 minutes loosely covered. Sprinkle with 15g/½oz cheese and bake for a further 20 minutes.

MICROWAVE: Place one portion on a suitable plate and microwave on DEFROST for 5 minutes. Sprinkle with 15g/½oz cheese and microwave on HIGH for 30 seconds.

Serving Suggestion:
Good served with grilled white fish and grilled tomatoes (count 10 calories each) or a portion of Mushrooms in Tomato Sauce (page xx).

MUSHROOM AND WINE PASTA SAUCE

Serves 8/60 calories per portion

10ml/2 level teaspoons low-fat spread
6 large spring onions, sliced
675g/1½lbs button mushrooms, sliced
30ml/2 level tablespoons flour
10ml/2 level teaspoons cornflour
150ml/¼ pint dry white wine
1½ vegetable stock cubes
850ml/1¼ pints water
30ml/2 level tablespoons parsley, chopped
10ml/2 level teaspoons dried thyme
Salt and pepper
40ml/8 level teaspoons Parmesan cheese, grated

1. Heat the low-fat spread in a pan. Add the onions, cover and cook for 2-3 minutes until softened.
2. Add the mushrooms to the pan. Replace lid and cook for 4-5 minutes, stirring occasionally.
3. Blend the flour and cornflour with the wine. Add to the vegetables along with the crumbled stock cubes, water, parsley, thyme, salt and pepper.
4. Bring to the boil, stirring continuously. Reduce the heat and simmer gently, uncovered, for 30-40 minutes until the sauce is thickened and glossy, stirring occasionally.

To Freeze:
Leave to cool at the end of stage 4. Divide into 8 portions, wrap, label and freeze.

To Serve:
CONVENTIONAL: Thaw at room temperature for 4 hours or overnight in a refrigerator. Reheat gently, stirring frequently, or reheat from frozen in a small pan over a low heat, stirring frequently. Sprinkle with Parmesan cheese.

MICROWAVE: Place one portion in a suitable bowl and microwave on DEFROST for 5 minutes. Microwave on HIGH for 1 minute. Sprinkle with Parmesan cheese.

Serving Suggestion:
This sauce is delicious with fresh wholemeal pasta such as tagliatelle. Allow 105 calories for 28g/1oz white pasta, weighed dry, or 95 calories for wholemeal pasta. If you are serving fresh pasta count 80 calories per 28g/1oz weighed before cooking.

QUICK-FRIED SWEET AND SOUR VEGETABLES

Serves 8/200 calories per portion

30ml/2 level tablespoons
cornflour
90ml/6 tablespoons wine
vinegar
60ml/4 tablespoons Soy
sauce
10ml/2 teaspoons
Worcestershire sauce
30ml/2 level tablespoons
honey
30ml/2 level tablespoons
tomato ketchup
30ml/2 tablespoons oil
2 red peppers, deseeded
and sliced
2 green peppers, deseeded
and sliced
225g/8oz carrots, cut into
thin diagonal slices
2 bulbs fennel, sliced
350g/12oz celery, cut into
short lengths
10 large spring onions,
trimmed and chopped
2 x 227g/8oz cans
pineapple pieces in
natural juice, drained,
juice reserved
115g/4oz cashew nuts

1. Blend the cornflour with the wine vinegar, Soy sauce, Worcestershire sauce, honey and ketchup.
2. Heat the oil in a wok or large frying pan. Add the peppers, carrots, fennel, celery and onions and cook, stirring continuously for 3 minutes.
3. Add the cornflour mixture and 6floz pineapple juice (made up with water if necessary), bring to the boil, simmer for 1 minute until it thickens and forms a glossy sauce.
4. Add the pineapple and nuts. Heat through for a few seconds, stirring.
5. Remove the vegetables from the pan to prevent further cooking.

To Freeze:
Cool at the end of stage 5. Divide into 8 portions, wrap, label and freeze.

To Serve:
CONVENTIONAL: Thaw at room temperature for 4 hours or overnight in a refrigerator. Put in a pan, cover and heat gently, stirring occasionally.

MICROWAVE: Put one portion in a suitable shallow dish and microwave on DEFROST for 10 minutes. Microwave on HIGH for 4 minutes.

Serving Suggestion:
This dish is good served with boiled rice. Allow 102 calories for 28g/1oz white rice, weighed dry, or 99 calories for brown rice. Alternatively, serve with boiled noodles. Allow 102 calories for 28g/1oz weighed dry.

CURRIED LENTIL DAHL

Serves 8/150 calories per portion

350g/12oz split red lentils
400g/14oz can tomatoes
2 medium onions, chopped
1 medium eating apple, peeled, cored and finely chopped
2 cloves garlic, crushed
10-20ml/2-4 level teaspoons curry paste, according to taste
1 bay leaf
15ml/1 level tablespoon mango chutney, large pieces chopped
30ml/2 tablespoons lemon juice
Salt and pepper

1. Wash the lentils in a sieve under cold running water. Drain and place in a large saucepan.
2. Purée the tomatoes and juice in a liquidizer or food processor, or rub through a sieve. Make up to 1 litre/1¾ pints with water and add to the lentils.
3. Add onions, apples, garlic, curry paste, bay leaf and mango chutney into the saucepan.
4. Cover the pan and bring to the boil. Stir well, cover and simmer gently for 30 minutes, stirring occasionally.
5. Add lemon juice and season to taste. Simmer gently, uncovered, stirring frequently until the mixture is a thick, quite dry consistency.
6. Remove the bay leaf.

To Freeze:
Leave to cool at the end of stage 6. Divide between 8 freezer containers or bags. Wrap, label and freeze.

To Serve:
CONVENTIONAL: Leave to thaw at room temperature for 2-3 hours or overnight in a refrigerator. Reheat gently in a small covered pan, stirring frequently.

MICROWAVE: Place one portion in a suitable dish and microwave on DEFROST for 7 minutes. Microwave on HIGH for 2 minutes.

Serving Suggestion:
This is an ideal side dish with any curry or Indian dish. It can also be served on its own (hot) with a crusty brown roll, allow 145 calories for a 45g/1¾oz roll or cold as a dip/starter with raw vegetables (crudites).

BRAISED MEDITERRANEAN VEGETABLES

Serves 8/105 calories per portion

350g/12oz courgettes,
thinly sliced
450g/1lb aubergines, cut
into cubes
Salt
15ml/1 tablespoon oil
1 red pepper, deseeded
and chopped
2 large onions, thinly
sliced
450g/1lb tomatoes, peeled
and chopped
2 cloves garlic, crushed
425g/15oz can borlotti
beans, drained
½ vegetable stock cube
150ml/¼ pint boiling
water
30ml/2 level tablespoons
tomato purée
5ml/1 level teaspoon dried
mixed herbs
Pepper

1. Place courgettes and aubergines in a colander and sprinkle with salt. Leave to stand for 30 minutes. Rinse, drain and pat dry with kitchen paper.
2. Grease a large casserole with the oil and place all the vegetables and beans in it.
3. Dissolve the stock cube in the boiling water and pour over the vegetables.
4. Stir the tomato purée and mixed herbs into the casserole, then season.
5. Cover and cook at 190ºC/375ºF, gas mark 5, for 1½ hours. Stir 2 or 3 times during cooking.

To Freeze:
Leave to cool at the end of stage 5. Divide into 8 portions, wrap, label and freeze.

To Serve:
CONVENTIONAL: Thaw for 4 hours at room temperature or overnight in a refrigerator. Reheat gently in a covered pan, stirring continuously.

MICROWAVE: Place in a suitable shallow container and microwave on DEFROST for 7 minutes. Microwave on HIGH for 1 minute. Stir before serving.

Serving Suggestion:
Serve as an accompaniment to meat or fish. A double portion would also make a light meal for 230 calories. Sprinkle the top with 25g/1oz reduced-fat Cheddar cheese and it will add 80 calories.

POTATO AND SWEET PEPPER GRATIN

Serves 8/235 calories per portion

1.15kg/2½lbs potatoes, peeled weight, cut into 2cm/1 inch chunks
Salt
40g/1½oz low-fat spread
2 medium onions, chopped
1 red pepper, deseeded and chopped
1 green pepper, deseeded and chopped
1-2 green chillies, deseeded and finely chopped
40g/1½oz wholemeal flour
½ vegetable stock cube
425ml/¾ pint water
425ml/¾ pint skimmed milk
45ml/3 level tablespoons cornflour
50g/2oz reduced-fat Cheddar cheese, grated
Pepper
40g/1½oz sesame seeds

1. Cook the potatoes in boiling, salted water until just tender. Drain.
2. Heat 15g/½oz low-fat spread in a non-stick pan. Add the onions, peppers and chilli. Cover and cook over a low heat for 5-7 minutes until soft but not mushy, stirring occasionally.
3. Reserve 5ml/1 level teaspoon low-fat spread, then place the remainder in a pan with the flour, crumbled stock cube, water and 275ml/½ pint skimmed milk. Bring to the boil, then simmer for 1 minute, stirring all the time.
4. Blend the cornflour with the remaining milk, until smooth. Whisk into the sauce and heat until boiling again. Simmer for 1-2 minutes, whisking continuously. Remove from the heat.
5. Stir in the cheese, salt and pepper.
6. Grease eight ovenproof freezer dishes with the reserved low-fat spread. Divide the potato between the dishes. Top with the onion mixture.
7. Pour the sauce over the vegetables and sprinkle with sesame seeds.

To Freeze:
Leave to cool at the end of stage 7, wrap, label and freeze.

To Serve:
CONVENTIONAL: Reheat from frozen at 200°C/400°F, gas mark 6, for 1¼ hours. Or, thaw at room temperature for 4 hours or overnight in a refrigerator. Reheat at 190°C/375°F, gas mark 5, for 30-40 minutes.

MICROWAVE: Microwave on DEFROST for 25 minutes. Microwave on HIGH for 5 minutes.

Serving Suggestion:
This dish is good served with white fish or chicken — alternatively it makes a filling lunch dish on its own.

MUSHROOMS IN TOMATO SAUCE

Serves 8/45 calories per portion

2 × 425g/15oz cans tomatoes
2 medium onions, chopped
2 cloves garlic, crushed
60ml/4 level tablespoons tomato ketchup
2 carrots, chopped
2 sticks celery, chopped
10ml/2 level teaspoons honey
10ml/2 level teaspoons tomato purée
450g/1lb mushrooms, halved if large
20ml/4 level teaspoons fresh basil
Salt and pepper

1. Put the tomatoes and their juice into a pan along with the onions, garlic, tomato ketchup, carrots, celery, honey and tomato purée.
2. Bring to the boil, stirring to break up the tomatoes, simmer partially covered for 20-25 minutes.
3. Remove from the heat and rub through a sieve or blend in a liquidizer or food processor.
4. Return the tomato sauce along with the mushrooms, basil, salt and pepper to the pan and simmer rapidly uncovered for 10 minutes until the sauce is thick and pulpy, stirring occasionally.

To Freeze:
Leave to cool at the end of stage 4. Divide into 8 portions, wrap, label and freeze.

To Serve:
CONVENTIONAL: Unwrap and reheat gently from frozen in a small covered pan with 15ml/1 tablespoon water, stirring occasionally.

MICROWAVE: Place in a suitable shallow dish and microwave on DEFROST for 5 minutes. Microwave on HIGH for 2 minutes. Stir before serving.

Serving Suggestion:
This dish is good served with grilled steak. Allow 320 calories for a 175g/6oz raw weight rump steak, medium-grilled. Also good with Cheesy Rice Filled Courgettes (page 117).

CREAMY BUTTER BEAN PURÉE

Serves 8/150 calories per portion

350g/12oz dried butter beans or 3×425g/15oz cans butter beans
10ml/2 level teaspoons low-fat spread
1 leek or 6 large spring onions, finely sliced
25g/1oz pine nuts or almonds, toasted
30ml/2 level tablespoons soured cream
45ml/3 level tablespoons low-fat natural yogurt
15ml/1 level tablespoon lemon juice
Salt and pepper

1. If using dried beans, cover with cold water and soak overnight. Drain off the water and cover with fresh unsalted water, bring to the boil, cover and simmer for 1½-1¾ hours until the beans are tender. If using canned beans, drain.
2. Heat the low-fat spread in a non-stick pan and gently fry the leek or onions, covered, for 4-5 minutes until soft.
3. Purée the cooked beans in a food processor until smooth or mash well with a potato masher.
4. Add the leeks or onions, nuts, soured cream, yogurt and lemon juice to the beans. Season to taste.

To Freeze:
Divide into eight. Place on a foil-lined baking tray and open freeze. Wrap, label and return to the freezer.

To Serve:
CONVENTIONAL: Thaw at room temperature for 4 hours or overnight in a refrigerator. Place one portion onto a square of foil and wrap loosely. Reheat at 190°C/375°F, gas mark 5, for 25 minutes, or place one portion onto a square of foil, wrap loosely and reheat from frozen at 200°C/400°F, gas mark 6, for 50-55 minutes.

MICROWAVE: Place one portion on a suitable plate and microwave on DEFROST for 15 minutes. Microwave on HIGH for 4 minutes.

Serving Suggestion:
Good served with any roast meats.

BARBECUED BEAN HOTPOT

Serves 8/265 calories per portion

450g/1lb soya beans
2.2litres/4 pints cold water
1 vegetable stock cube
725ml/1¼ pints boiling water
150ml/¼ pint apple juice
2 medium onions, chopped
60ml/4 level tablespoons tomato purée
60ml/4 tablespoons Soy sauce
20ml/4 level teaspoons honey
45ml/3 tablespoons cider or wine vinegar
15ml/1 level tablespoon mustard powder
2 cloves garlic, crushed
30ml/2 level tablespoons cornflour
Salt and pepper

1. Soak the beans in cold water for at least 12 hours. Put them in a saucepan, bring to the boil and simmer for 3 hours. Drain.
2. Place the beans into a large casserole.
3. Dissolve the stock cube in the boiling water and pour over the beans along with the apple juice, onions, tomato purée, Soy sauce, honey, vinegar, mustard and garlic.
4. Blend the cornflour with a little cold water and stir into the casserole.
5. Cover and cook at 180°C/350°F, gas mark 4, for 2 hours.
6. Season with salt and pepper.

To Freeze:
Cool at the end of stage 6. Divide into 8 portions, wrap, label and freeze.

To Serve:
CONVENTIONAL: Thaw at room temperature for 4 hours overnight in a refrigerator. Place in a saucepan; reheat gently stirring frequently.

MICROWAVE: Place one portion in a suitable dish and microwave on DEFROST for 5 minutes. Microwave on HIGH for 1 minute. Stir before serving.

Serving Suggestion:
Serve with boiled rice and a crisp green salad. Allow 102 calories for 28g/1oz white rice, weighed dry, or 99 calories for brown rice. A green salad will cost about 25 calories without dressing.

MIXED VEGETABLE STIR FRY

Serves 4/145 calories per portion

30ml/2 tablespoons dry sherry
45ml/3 tablespoons Soy sauce
1-2 drops Tabasco sauce
30ml/2 level tablespoons tomato ketchup
15ml/1 tablespoon Worcestershire sauce
15ml/1 level tablespoon cornflour
20ml/4 teaspoons oil
1 medium onion, thinly sliced
175g/6oz carrots, cut into thin matchsticks
150g/5oz broccoli florets, weighed with large woody stalks removed, cut into small florets
115g/4oz button mushrooms, thinly sliced
198g/7oz can sweetcorn, drained

1. Make the sauce by blending the dry sherry, Soy sauce, Tabasco sauce, ketchup, Worcestershire sauce and cornflour together. Set aside.
2. Heat the oil in a wok or large frying pan. Stir fry the onion for 2 minutes.
3. Add the carrots, broccoli and mushrooms to the pan. Stir fry over a high heat for 3 minutes.
4. Add the sweetcorn and heat through.
5. Pour over the sauce and bring to the boil, stirring. Remove vegetables from the pan to prevent further cooking.

To Freeze:
Cool at the end of stage 5, divide between 4 bags or freezer containers, wrap, label and freeze.

To Serve:
CONVENTIONAL: Thaw at room temperature for 3-4 hours or overnight in a refrigerator. Reheat gently in a small pan with 15ml/1 tablespoon water, uncovered, stirring occasionally until bubbling. Do not overcook.

MICROWAVE: Place in a suitable dish and microwave on DEFROST for 10 minutes. Add 15ml/1 tablespoon water and microwave on HIGH for 1 minute. Stir before serving.

Serving Suggestion:
This rich tasty stir fry is delicious with lean roast beef or grilled steak. Allow 50 calories per 28g/1oz serving topside, lean only or 48 calories per 28g/1oz rump steak, grilled, lean only.

VEGETARIAN MOUSSAKA

Serves 8/265 calories per portion

450g/1lb aubergines, stems removed and sliced
Salt
3 large onions, sliced
2 x 425g/15oz cans tomatoes
30ml/2 level tablespoons tomato purée
5ml/1 level teaspoon dried thyme
10ml/2 level teaspoons ground coriander
½ vegetable stock cube
175ml/6floz water
1.35kg/3lbs potatoes, peeled weight, sliced
40g/1½oz low-fat spread
40g/1½oz wholemeal flour
850ml/1½ pints skimmed milk
30ml/2 level tablespoons cornflour
2 eggs, size 3, beaten
Pepper

1. Place the aubergines in a colander and sprinkle with salt. Leave to stand for 30 minutes. Rinse, drain and pat dry with kitchen paper.
2. Meanwhile put the onions, tomatoes and their juice, tomato purée, thyme, coriander, crumbled stock cube and water in a pan.
3. Bring to the boil, stirring to break up the tomatoes and simmer uncovered for 20-25 minutes, until thick and pulpy.
4. Boil the sliced potatoes until partly cooked. Drain.
5. Grease 8 small ovenproof freezer containers using 5ml/1 level teaspoon low-fat spread.
6. Layer the aubergine slices, tomato mixture and potato slices alternately into the containers.
7. Place the remaining low-fat spread, flour and 725ml/1¼ pints skimmed milk in a pan. Bring to the boil, whisking all the time, then simmer for 1 minute.
8. Blend the cornflour with the remaining milk until smooth. Whisk into the sauce and heat until boiling again.
9. Remove from the heat and beat in the eggs. Season.
10. Pour sauce over the top of the aubergine, tomato and potato layers.
11. Bake at 200°C/400°F, gas mark 6, for 1-1¼ hours or until the top is set.

To Freeze:
Leave to cool at the end of stage 11, wrap, label and freeze.

To Serve:
CONVENTIONAL: Thaw for 4 hours at room temperature or overnight in a refrigerator. Loosely cover with foil and reheat at 190°C/375°F, gas mark 5, for 1 hour.

MICROWAVE: Place in a suitable dish and microwave on DEFROST for 20 minutes. Microwave on HIGH for 2 minutes.

Serving Suggestion:
You can serve this moussaka on its own or add a few salad vegetables — iceberg lettuce would be good and cost you under 20 calories a serving.

VEGETABLE CURRY

Serves 8/200 calories per portion

175g/6oz red lentils,
washed
450g/1lb carrots, peeled
and sliced
225g/8oz swede, peeled
and cubed
2 leeks, washed and
chopped
450g/1lb cauliflower
florets
1.2 litres/2 pints water
2 stock cubes, vegetable or
chicken
30ml/2 level tablespoons
mild curry powder
10ml/2 level teaspoons salt
Ground black pepper
450g/1lb broad beans,
frozen
200g/7oz can sweetcorn,
drained

1. Place all ingredients except broad beans and sweetcorn in a large saucepan.
2. Cover and simmer for 15 minutes.
3. Add broad beans and sweetcorn and cook for a further 10 minutes.

To Freeze:
Divide curry between 8 polythene bags, seal, label and freeze.

To Serve:
CONVENTIONAL: Defrost overnight in a refrigerator and pour into a saucepan. Reheat over a low heat.
To reheat from frozen: place in a saucepan over a low heat and slowly heat through, stirring occasionally.

MICROWAVE: Microwave on DEFROST for 7½ minutes. Stir occasionally. Microwave on HIGH for 3 minutes.

Serving Suggestion:
Serve as an accompaniment to chicken or pork. Serve alone with boiled rice.

RICE AND PEPPER AU GRATIN

Serves 8/195 calories per portion

175g/6oz long-grain brown rice
1 red pepper, deseeded and diced
1 green pepper, deseeded and diced
4 sticks celery, chopped
15ml/1 tablespoon oil
425g/15oz can tomatoes
Pinch chilli powder
Salt and pepper
175g/6oz mature Cheddar cheese, grated

1. Cook rice as instructed n the packet.
2. Fry peppers and celery in oil until soft but not brown.
3. Stir in tomatoes and their juice, chilli powder and seasoning.
4. Add cooked rice and simmer for 10 minutes or until thick.

To Freeze:
Divide between 8 individual freezer containers and cool. Sprinkle cheese on top. Seal, label and freeze.

To Serve:
CONVENTIONAL: Reheat in a covered dish at 200°C/400°F, gas mark 6, for 45 minutes. Brown cheese under a grill, OR defrost overnight in the refrigerator and reheat at 200°C/400°F, gas mark 6 for 20-30 minutes or until hot and brown cheese under a grill.

MICROWAVE: Microwave on DEFROST for 5 minutes. Microwave on HIGH for 3 minutes or until hot.

Serving Suggestion:
On its own or accompanied with a salad.

CELERIAC AND POTATO PURÉE

Serves 8/75 calories per portion

450g/1lb celeriac, peeled weight
450g/1lb old potatoes, peeled weight
Salt and pepper
1 egg, size 3
1 egg yolk, size 3

1. Cut the celeriac and potatoes into even-sized pieces, then cook in boiling water for 10-15 minutes, until tender. Drain well, then mash until smooth.
2. Season with salt and pepper.
3. Lightly beat the whole egg and extra yolk together, then beat into the celeriac and potato mixture.
4. Line a baking sheet with foil. Pipe or spoon the purée into 16 pyramid shapes and leave to cool.

To Freeze:
Open freeze until solid. Pack two pyramids into each freezer bag, label and return to the freezer.

To Serve:
CONVENTIONAL: Place one portion (two pyramids) on a non-stick tin and bake at 200°C/400°F, gas mark 6, for 25 minutes.

MICROWAVE: Place one portion on a suitable plate and microwave on DEFROST for 5 minutes. Microwave on HIGH for 2 minutes.

Serving Suggestion:
Delicious with roast or grilled meats.

FESTIVE-STYLE VEGETABLES

Serves 8/145 calories per portion

115g/4oz dried chestnuts
Salt
900g/2lb Brussels sprouts, washed and halved
175g/6oz carrots, cut into matchsticks
40ml/8 teaspoons oil
40ml/8 level teaspoons low-fat spread
Pepper

1. Soak the chestnuts overnight by pouring boiling water over and leaving them for 12 hours. Drain and place in a saucepan of fresh salted water and bring to the boil. Simmer until the chestnuts are tender, about 20-40 minutes. Drain. Cut in half.
2. Blanch the Brussels sprouts in boiling water for 3 minutes. Drain and rinse under ice-cold water and pat dry on kitchen paper.
3. Blanch the carrots in boiling water for 2 minutes. Drain and rinse under ice-cold water and pat dry on kitchen paper.
4. Mix the vegetables with the chestnuts and divide between eight freezer containers or bags.

To Freeze:
Wrap, label and freeze.

To Serve:
CONVENTIONAL: Heat 5ml/1 teaspoon oil and 5ml/1 level teaspoon low-fat spread in a small pan. Add the vegetables, salt and pepper and fry over a high heat for 4-5 minutes until heated through, stirring occasionally to prevent sticking.

MICROWAVE: Not suitable.

Serving Suggestion:
This is good served with roast meats especially turkey and it is also nice with boiled or baked gammon.

CURRIED VEGETABLE PIE

Serves 8/175 calories

2 medium onions,
chopped
175g/6oz celery, sliced
225g/8oz carrots, chopped
2½ cm/1 inch piece root
ginger, peeled and finely
chopped
1 vegetable or chicken
stock cube
850ml/1½ pints boiling
water
45ml/3 level tablespoons
tomato purée
45ml/3 tablespoons lemon
juice
45ml/3 level tablespoons
mango chutney
20ml/4 level teaspoons
curry paste
425g/15oz can brown or
red kidney beans
350g/12oz cauliflower
florets
175g/6oz courgettes,
sliced
60ml/4 tablespoons cold
water
Salt and pepper
900g/2lb potatoes, peeled
weight
1 egg, size 3
30ml/2 tablespoons
skimmed milk

1. Put onions, celery, carrots and ginger in a large pan.
2. Dissolve the stock cube in the water and pour over the vegetables.
3. Add the tomato purée, lemon juice, mango chutney (chopping any large pieces) and curry paste.
4. Bring to the boil, cover and simmer for 10 minutes.
5. Add the beans, cauliflower and courgettes. Cook for a further 10 minutes.
6. Blend the cornflour with the water and add to the pan. Bring to the boil, stirring and simmer for 1-2 minutes. Season.
7. Divide between eight small freezer containers.
8. Cut potatoes into even-sized chunks and boil until tender. Drain.
9. Lightly beat egg and milk together. Mash with the potato. Season with salt and pepper. Spread over the vegetable mixture.

To Freeze:
Cool at the end of stage 9, open freeze until solid. Wrap, label and return to the freezer.

To Serve:
CONVENTIONAL: Reheat from frozen at 220°C/425°F, gas mark 7, for 1-1¼ hours.

MICROWAVE: Put one portion in a suitable dish and DEFROST for 20 minutes. Cook on HIGH for 7 minutes or until hot.

Serving Suggestion:
Can be served on its own or if you wish, add a few boiled runner beans (7 calories per 28g/1oz weighed raw).

NUTTY RAINBOW RICE

Serves 8/175 calories per portion

2 medium onions, chopped
2 cloves garlic, crushed
225g/8oz long-grain brown rice
7.5ml/1 ½ level teaspoons salt
Pepper
575ml/1 pint water
115g/4oz carrots, chopped
175g/6oz French beans, cut into 2cm/1 inch lengths
1 small red pepper, deseeded and chopped
115g/4oz canned sweetcorn
50g/2oz hazelnuts, toasted and chopped
30ml/2 level tablespoons parsley, chopped

1. Put onions, garlic, rice, salt, pepper and water in a saucepan.
2. Cover the pan and bring to the boil. Stir well. Cover and simmer gently for 40 minutes.
3. Meanwhile cook the carrot, beans and pepper for 3 minutes in boiling water. Drain.
4. When cooked the rice should be tender and all the liquid absorbed. If there is any excess liquid cook uncovered for a few minutes to allow it to evaporate.
5. Gently stir in the cooked vegetables along with the sweetcorn, hazelnuts, parsley and rice using a fork.
6. Replace the lid and remove from the heat. Leave to stand for 10 minutes.

To Freeze:
Cool at the end of stage 6. Divide into 8 portions, wrap, label and freeze.

To Serve:
CONVENTIONAL: Thaw at room temperature for 3-4 hours or overnight in a refrigerator. Place in a pan with 15ml/1 tablespoon water, cover and heat gently stirring occasionally.

MICROWAVE: Put one portion in a suitable shallow dish and microwave on DEFROST for 10 minutes. Microwave on HIGH for 2 minutes. Stir before serving.

Serving Suggestion:
This dish can be served hot or cold and is good as an accompaniment to baked fish or casseroled meat.

MOORISH-STYLE RICE

Serves 8/170 calories per portion

2 medium onions, chopped
Finely grated rind of 1 lemon
225g/8oz long-grain brown rice
1 vegetable stock cube
575ml/1 pint water
2.5ml/½ level teaspoon turmeric
10ml/2 level teaspoons mixed spice
5ml/1 level teaspoon salt
Pepper
75g/3oz ready-to-eat dried apricots, soaked and chopped
40g/1½oz stoned dates, chopped
50g/2oz walnuts, chopped

1. Put onions and lemon rind in a saucepan with the rice, crumbled stock cube, water, turmeric, mixed spice, salt and pepper.
2. Cover the pan and bring to the boil. Stir well, cover and simmer gently for 40 minutes. Stir occasionally and if rice starts to stick add a little extra water.
3. When cooked the rice should be tender and all the water absorbed. If there is any excess liquid cook uncovered for a few minutes to allow it to evaporate.
4. Gently stir the apricots, dates and walnuts into the pan.
5. Replace the lid and remove from the heat. Leave to stand for 10 minutes.

To Freeze:
Cool at the end of stage 5. Divide into 8 portions, wrap, label and freeze.

To Serve:
CONVENTIONAL: Thaw at room temperature for 3-4 hours or overnight in a refrigerator. Put in a pan with 15ml/1 tablespoon water, cover and heat gently, stirring occasionally.

MICROWAVE: Put one portion in a suitable shallow dish and microwave on DEFROST for 5 minutes. Microwave on HIGH for 1 minute. Stir before serving.

Serving Suggestion:
This is delicious as an accompaniment to fish, especially trout and mackerel.

CHEESY VEGETABLE LAYER CRUMBLE

Serves 8/315 calories per portion

900g/2lb potatoes, peeled weight, thinly sliced
15ml/1 tablespoon oil
675g/1½lbs onions, thinly sliced
350g/12oz celery, chopped
10ml/2 level teaspoons low-fat spread
225g/8oz reduced fat Cheddar cheese, grated
425ml/¾ pint low-fat natural yogurt
150ml/¼ pint soured cream
Salt and pepper
115g/4oz fresh wholemeal breadcrumbs
Pinch cayenne pepper
8 medium tomatoes, thinly sliced

1. Boil the sliced potatoes for a few minutes until partly cooked. Drain.
2. Heat the oil in a pan and add the onions and celery. Cover and cook vegetables over a low heat for 10 minutes, or until tender but not mushy.
3. Grease 8 small ovenproof freezer containers using the low-fat spread.
4. Layer half the potatoes, onions and celery and one-third of the cheese in the containers. Repeat these layers.
5. Mix the yogurt, soured cream, salt and pepper and pour over the vegetables.
6. Combine the remaining cheese with the breadcrumbs and cayenne pepper and sprinkle on top of the sauce.
7. Cook at 180°C/350°F, gas mark 4, for 1 hour, or until tender.

To Freeze:
Leave to cool at the end of stage 7, wrap, label and freeze.

To Serve:
CONVENTIONAL: Thaw at room temperature for 4 hours or overnight in a refrigerator. Reheat at 180°C/350°F, gas mark 4, for 20 minutes. Add one sliced tomato on top and return to the oven for 15-20 minutes until crispy and golden.

MICROWAVE: Place dish in microwave and cook on DEFROST for 20 minutes. Cook on HIGH for 2 minutes.

Serving Suggestion:
Cheesy Vegetable Layer Crumble can be eaten on its own or with a green salad.

APPLE AND POTATO SAVOURIES

Serves 8/90 calories per portion

1 medium cooking apple,
    peeled and sliced
450g/1lb potatoes, peeled
    weight and thinly sliced
225g/8oz cabbage, finely
    sliced
15ml/1 level tablespoon
    low-fat yogurt
1 egg, size 3, beaten
Salt and pepper
75g/3oz fresh wholemeal
    breadcrumbs

1. Cook the apple and potatoes in boiling, salted water for 5-7 minutes until tender. Drain well and replace over a low heat, uncovered, until thoroughly dry. Beat until smooth.
2. Cook the cabbage in boiling, salted water until just tender. Drain.
3. Mix the apple and potato with the yogurt, half of the egg, salt and pepper.
4. Stir in the cooked cabbage. Cool.
5. Divide into eight and shape into flat cakes. Coat in the remaining egg and breadcrumbs.

To Freeze:
Place on a foil-lined baking tray and open freeze until solid. Wrap, label and freeze.

To Serve:
CONVENTIONAL: Place one portion on a lightly greased baking tray and cook from frozen at 200°C/400°F, gas mark 6, for 40-50 minutes, turning halfway through cooking time.

MICROWAVE: Place one portion on a suitable plate and microwave on DEFROST for 15 minutes. Microwave on HIGH for 4 minutes.

Serving Suggestion:
Serve with grilled pork sausages — allow 125 calories for each large, well-grilled sausage.

PUDDINGS TO FREEZE

Home-made ice creams and sorbets are delicious and any of the recipes included in this section would make a low calorie ending to a meal. And there are other fruity desserts that are worth making to keep in the freezer, too. Also in this chapter are cakes and teabreads that can either be eaten as a dessert or as a tea-time treat. Always cut cake or teabread into slices before freezing, and wrap each slice individually in freezer film. That means you won't have to defrost the lot in one go. One of the biggest temptations for any sweet-toothed slimmer is a big cake sitting in the kitchen just asking you to cut another slice, then another...

INDIVIDUAL SUMMER PUDS

Serves 8/160 calories per portion

275g/10oz crustless white sliced bread
450g/1lb redcurrants, stalks removed
225g/8oz raspberries
115g/4oz strawberries, stalks removed
115g/4oz caster sugar

1. Rinse eight plastic-lidded cartons (small yogurt or cottage cheese cartons are ideal). Set aside.
2. Cut 16 circles of bread using the base of a carton as a template.
3. Use 8 circles to line the bases of the cartons, reserve the remainder. With the trimmings cut rectangles and triangles and use to line the sides of the cartons. Make sure there are no gaps and the bread comes to the top edge of each carton.
4. Wash the prepared fruit and put into a saucepan with the sugar. Cook gently, covered, for 5 minutes or until the fruit is softened but not mushy and some of the juices have been extracted.
5. Spoon the hot fruit into the lined cartons and spoon over the juice.
6. Cover each pudding with one of the 8 remaining circles of bread. Replace the carton top — it should be a tight fit.
7. Put a weight on top of each, such as a full jam jar and leave overnight in a refrigerator.

To Freeze:
Remove the weights. Label and freeze.

To Serve:
Thaw at room temperature for 3-4 hours or overnight in a refrigerator. Remove the lid and loosen the edges of the pudding with a knife. Place a small plate over the carton and invert the pudding onto a plate.

Serving Suggestion:
Mix 15ml/1 level tablespoon soured cream with 15ml/1 level tablespoon low-fat yogurt and spoon over the pudding. This will cost an extra 40 calories.

ORANGE FLUFF

Serves 8/100 calories per portion

2 x 127g/4½ oz packets orange-flavoured jelly
150ml/¼ pint boiling water
150ml/5floz low-fat natural yogurt
4 egg whites, size 3

1. Cut jelly into cubes and place in a saucepan with the boiling water. Stand over a low heat until jelly dissolves.
2. Pour into a measuring jug and make up to 850ml/1½ pints with cold water. Place in a refrigerator until just beginning to set.
3. Whip egg whites until stiff.
4. Turn jelly into a large bowl and whisk in yogurt until frothy. Fold in egg whites.
5. When smooth and well blended, transfer into 8 individual containers — individual yogurt cartons are ideal.

To Freeze:
Cover, label and freeze.

To Serve:
Thaw at room temperature for 3-4 hours, or overnight in the refrigerator.

Serving Suggestion:
Serve from frozen in the individual cartons or scooped into serving glasses.

THREE FRUIT TEABREAD

Makes 12 slices/130 calories per slice

275ml/½ pint freshly made Earl Grey tea
50g/2oz dried apricots, chopped
50g/2oz sultanas
25g/1oz stoneless prunes, chopped
2 eggs, size 3
30ml/2 tablespoons corn oil
45ml/3 level tablespoons clear honey
115ml/4floz buttermilk
225g/8oz wholemeal self-raising flour
5ml/1 level teaspoon baking powder
Finely grated rind ½ lemon

1. Soak the dried fruit in the tea overnight, then drain, discarding tea.
2. Line a non-stick 1kg/2lb loaf tin with greaseproof paper.
3. Beat eggs, oil, honey and buttermilk together in a bowl. Sift in the flour and baking powder, adding any bran remaining in the sieve. Stir in the lemon rind and fruit in tea.
4. Bake at 190°C/375°F, gas mark 5 for 60-70 minutes or until a fine skewer inserted comes out clean. Leave to cool in the tin for 10 minutes. Remove from tin, but leave until cold before discarding the lining paper.

To Freeze:
Cut the cake into 12 slices. Wrap each one individually, label and freeze.

To Serve:
CONVENTIONAL: Leave to thaw at room temperature for 1-2 hours.

MICROWAVE: DEFROST for 5 minutes. Microwave on HIGH for 1½ minutes.

BANANA, DATE AND WALNUT BREAD

Makes 16 slices/90 calories per slice

275ml/½ pint skimmed milk
25g/1oz honey
75g/3oz All Bran
175g/6oz wholemeal self-raising flour
7.5ml/1½ teaspoons baking powder
450g/1lb ripe bananas, mashed
50g/2oz stoned dates, chopped
25g/1oz walnuts, chopped
15-30ml/1-2 tablespoons skimmed milk

1. Heat 275ml/½ pint milk and the honey in a pan until the honey has dissolved. Put the All Bran in a bowl, pour over the milk and leave to soak overnight.
2. Line a non-stick 1kg/2lb loaf tin or 2×450g/1lb loaf tins with greaseproof paper.
3. Sift the flour and baking powder into the moist cereal mixture, adding any bran remaining in the sieve. Stir in the fruit and nuts until well blended, adding enough milk to give a soft dropping consistency.
4. Spoon the mixture into the prepared tin(s) and bake at 190°C/375°F, gas mark 5 for 1 hour (1kg/2lb tin) or 1¼ hours (2×450g/1lb) until a fine skewer inserted comes out clean. Leave to cool in the tin for 10 minutes before turning out. Remove the lining paper when the cake is cold.

To Freeze:
Divide into 16 slices. Wrap individually, label and freeze.

To Serve:
CONVENTIONAL: Thaw a slice at room temperature for 1-2 hours. If you wish spread with 2.5ml/½ level teaspoon low-fat spread which adds an extra 5 calories.

MICROWAVE: DEFROST for 5 minutes; then microwave on HIGH for 1½ minutes. Serve with low-fat spread as above.

CHOCOLATE AND BANANA ICE CREAM

Serves 8/160 calories per portion

450g/1lb ripe bananas, weighed with skins
15ml/1 tablespoon lemon juice
400g/14oz can evaporated milk, chilled overnight
25g/1oz cocoa powder
15ml/1 tablespoon boiling water
75g/3oz icing sugar, sifted

1. Peel the bananas and purée them in a food processor or liquidizer until smooth. Stir in the lemon juice.
2. Whisk the chilled evaporated milk until it becomes thick and frothy.
3. Mix the cocoa with the water; add the milk along with the banana mixture and blend until smooth.
4. Fold the sugar, gently, into the mixture.
5. Pour into a freezer container and freeze. After 1 hour take ice cream from freezer and beat well. Return to the freezer for a further hour, then beat again.
6. Divide between eight individual cartons.

To Freeze:
Wrap, label and freeze.

To Serve:
Serve frozen in the container or scooped into a dish.

STRAWBERRY AND COINTREAU SORBET

Serves 8/145 calories per portion

450g/1lb fresh strawberries, washed and stalks removed
Juice of 1 lemon
Juice of 1 orange
30ml/2 tablespoons Cointreau
225g/8oz caster sugar
275ml/½ pint water
2 egg whites, size 3

1. Crush the strawberries or purée in a liquidizer or food processor. Rub through a sieve to remove seeds.
2. Stir the lemon juice, orange juice and Cointreau into the strawberry pulp.
3. Put the sugar and water into a pan and stir over a low heat, until the sugar is dissolved, bring to the boil. Remove from heat and stir into the strawberry mixture. Leave until cold.
4. Pour the mixture into a freezer container. Freeze uncovered until icy at the edges.
5. Whisk the egg whites until soft peaks form.
6. Fold the egg whites into the strawberry mixture until thick and light.
7. Divide between 8 small cartons or containers and return uncovered to the freezer.

To Freeze:
When firm, cover with a lid or film.

To Serve:
Eat frozen from container or scooped into a serving glass.

BLACKCURRANT SYLLABUB

Serves 4/300 calories per portion

115g/4oz cottage cheese
150ml/5floz double cream
50g/2oz caster sugar
Rind and juice of ½ lemon
45ml/3 tablespoons dry
white wine
50g/2oz fresh or frozen
blackcurrants
30ml/2 level tablespoons
low-fat natural yogurt
Grated rind ½ lemon
8 sponge fingers

1. Sieve the cottage cheese and place in a food processor or liquidizer along with the cream, sugar, lemon rind and juice and wine. Blend until thick and light.
2. Purée and sieve the blackcurrants and add to the syllabub with the yogurt. Blend together until light, and of a consistency to hold its shape. Spoon into individual tall glasses (wine glasses are ideal). Leave uncovered in the refrigerator to chill for 2-3 hours.
3. Decorate before serving with the rind of lemon. Serve with sponge fingers.

RASPBERRY AND REDCURRANT ICE CREAM

Serves 8/145 calories per portion

400g/14oz can evaporated
milk, chilled overnight
225g/8oz fresh
raspberries, washed
225g/8oz fresh
redcurrants, stalks
removed and washed
115g/4oz icing sugar, sifted

1. Whisk the chilled evaporated milk until it becomes thick and frothy.
2. Purée the raspberries and redcurrants in a liquidizer or food processor. Rub through a sieve to remove seeds.
3. Stir the icing sugar into the evaporated milk then stir in the fruit.
4. Pour into a freezer container and freeze for 1 hour. Beat well, then return to the freezer for a further hour. Beat again, then divide between 8 equal-sized cartons or containers.

To Freeze:
Wrap, label and freeze until solid.

To Serve:
Serve from frozen in the cartons or scooped out into serving glasses.

CARROT CAKE

Makes 8 slices/190 calories per slice

115g/4oz cottage cheese
50g/2oz soft light brown
sugar
1 egg, size 3, lightly
beaten
115g/4oz carrots, grated
115g/4oz sultanas
Grated rind and juice 1
medium orange
5ml/1 level teaspoon
ground cinnamon
200g/7oz granary flour
10ml/2 level teaspoons
baking powder
5ml/1 teaspoon corn oil

1. Sieve the cottage cheese into a bowl and cream with the sugar until light and creamy. Add the egg a little at a time, beating well after each addition.
2. Stir in the carrot, sultanas, orange rind and cinnamon until well blended. Sift in the granary flour and baking powder, adding any bran remaining in the sieve. Stir in the orange juice to give a moist, soft consistency, adding a little hot water if necessary.
3. Lightly grease a 18cm/7 inch round cake tin with the oil and line the base with non-stick baking paper. Spoon the mixture into the prepared tin and bake at 190°C/375°F, gas mark 5 for 1 hour, or until a skewer inserted in the middle comes out clean. Leave in the tin for 10 minutes before turning out. Remove the greaseproof paper when nearly cold.

To Freeze:
Cut into 8 wedges. Wrap, label and freeze.

To Serve:
CONVENTIONAL: Leave to thaw at room temperature for 1-2 hours.

MICROWAVE: DEFROST for 5 minutes. Microwave on HIGH for 1½ minutes.